Post-Conflict Environmental Assessment

Afghanistan

This report by the United Nations Environment Programme was made possible by the generous contribution of the governments of Canada, Finland, Luxembourg and Switzerland

Table of Contents

Foreword

The year 2002 brought hope for peace, stability and reconstruction in Afghanistan. It was the year that saw the massive return of refugees to the country, the first *Loya Jirga* in decades, and impressive financial assistance from the international community.

It was also the year when Afghans started rebuilding their country with resolute determination. Facing huge reconstruction challenges, this war-torn society showed exceptional leadership and dedication in establishing post-conflict policies and institutions.

Decades of conflict and violence coupled with drought and earthquakes have had devastating impacts not only the people of Afghanistan, but also on its natural environment, once pristine and rich in biological diversity, but now suffering from years of overexploitation of natural resources and habitat loss.

It was clear from the outset that the United Nations Environment Programme (UNEP), as part of the overall response by the United Nations, would give its support to the people and authorities of Afghanistan by offering its expertise in post-conflict environmental assessment and analysis.

This report presents facts on the state of the environment, specific findings concerning the urban environment and the natural resources of Afghanistan and recommendations on how to improve environmental conditions and policies.

UNEP was able to meet this challenging task thanks to the close cooperation with the Ministry of Water Resources, Irrigation and Environment, and I extend my thanks to the Minister, Dr Ahmad Yusuf Nuristani, for his collaboration and strong commitment, and for the hard work by his staff. Moreover, the activities were planned in close coordination with the Afghan Assistance Coordination Agency (AACA) and the United Nations Assistance Mission to Afghanistan (UNAMA).

I am especially grateful to the governments of Canada, Finland, Luxembourg and Switzerland for having provided generous financial support for this assessment, and to all the environmental experts, both Afghan and international, who made the environmental assessment in Afghanistan possible.

I sincerely hope that this report will be useful not only to the people of Afghanistan, but also to all donor countries and international organizations looking for facts, figures and the vision needed during the reconstruction phase.

Klaus Töpfer
United Nations Under-Secretary General
Executive Director of the United Nations Environment Programme

Foreword

Afghanistan is at a crucial point in its tumultuous history. Since 1973, Afghanistan has changed regimes frequently, and has been led by eight different leaders. Instability and war has caused widespread devastation, insecurity, displacement, poverty and severe environmental degradation. After the tragic events of 11 September 2001 in the United States, Afghanistan received unprecedented international attention, and the events drew strong support for the required humanitarian, political and military actions and solutions needed to put Afghanistan on the road to peace, stability, recovery and development.

The Afghanistan Transitional Authority under the leadership of H.E. Mr. Hamid Karzai, is keen to see rapid change that will benefit the Afghan people. Serious efforts in the emergency relief and development sectors are crucial to assist Afghans in rebuilding lives worth living. Today, we are seeing many efforts dealing with the repatriation of returnees, provision of food security, private sector development and agricultural rehabilitation, as well as a proper education system and reliable health care. Environmental quality, protection and sustainable management of natural resources are the foundation on which all these dramatic improvements to our society need to be built.

It is tragic to see how many people have left Afghanistan due to war and drought-related issues. Apart from the conflict, environmental degradation has been an important force driving people to find a better future elsewhere. The lack of water resources has led to the collapse of many livelihoods, and most of the country is subject to an alarming degree of land degradation propelled by poverty, population growth and the need to survive. The country has also been robbed of its precious forest resources by Afghan and non-Afghan timber mafia and smugglers. The net result of the degradation is widespread desertification and erosion, and increased vulnerability to environmental disasters. Now is the time to take stock of the current conditions, develop systems for the sustainable use of resources and look for ways to rehabilitate degraded ecosystems.

UNEP's post-conflict environmental assessment illuminates Afghanistan's current levels of degradation, and sets forth a path that the country can take towards sustainable development. It warns us of a future without water, forests, wildlife, and clean air if environmental problems are not addressed in the reconstruction period. With the work that is presented to you in this document, UNEP has been instrumental in outlining the relationship between environment and development. The Afghan government will benefit greatly from this report as it develops the country's environmental policies and plans for rehabilitation. On behalf of the Afghan Transitional Authority, I urge readers to note carefully this report's priorities and recommendations, and to find the means and resources to put them into immediate practice.

Dr Ahmad Yusuf Nuristani
Minister of Irrigation, Water Resources and Environment
Afghanistan Transitional Authority

1

Loss of vegetation has caused serious soil erosion across the country, such as in this village near Mazar-e-Sharif

DENNIS BRUHN/UNEP 2002

Introduction

I n the capital of Afghanistan there is a saying: *May Kabul be without gold rather than without snow*. For most of the country's people the land, its biological resources and its ecological processes are the source of their livelihood and the foundation for their existence. Apart from the country's most arid deserts and frozen mountains, virtually the entire land surface of Afghanistan has been used for centuries – whether for local farming or, on a more wide-reaching basis, for livestock grazing, fuelwood collection and hunting.

Tragically, the combined pressures of warfare, civil disorder, lack of governance and drought have taken a major toll on Afghanistan's natural and human resources. These impacts have exacerbated a more general and long-standing process of land degradation, evidence of which is apparent throughout much of the country. As the country's natural resource base has declined, its vulnerability to natural disasters and food shortages has increased.

Clearly, effective natural resource management and rehabilitation must be a national priority if Afghanistan is to achieve long-term social stability and prosperity. Mitigation of environmental problems and protection of the environment will also support sustainable rural development and enhance job creation.

Background and scope of assessment

During the Bonn negotiations in late 2001, a new Afghanistan Interim Administration was formed. The international community expressed its readiness to support the new government of Afghanistan led by Chairman Hamid Karzai.

Post-Conflict Environmental Assessment

The high priorities of the new government have been to re-establish security and the rule of law, ensure the safe return of refugees and to assist internally displaced people. Humanitarian aid, new infrastructure and investments are now helping to create stability and income opportunities in Afghanistan.

Following the *Loya Jirga* in June 2002, the newly established Ministry for Irrigation, Water Resources and Environment was given a leadership role in integrating environmental recovery and rehabilitation into the reconstruction process. As environ-

Reconstructing Yakawalang village near Band-e-Amir

ment is always a cross-cutting issue, many other sector ministries, as well as regional and local levels of administration, also have key environmental obligations and responsibilities.

The scope of UNEP's post-conflict environmental assessment in Afghanistan has included such vital environmental issues as pollution 'hotspots' in the urban environment, surface and ground water resources, deforestation, waste and sanitation, air quality, and desertification. The status of various protected areas was also investigated. Environmen-

> **Afghanistan administrative boundaries and main cities**

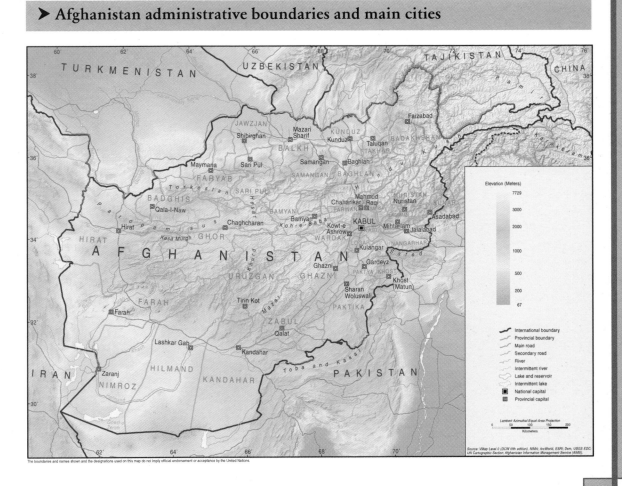

tal improvements cannot be made without proper institutional arrangements. Therefore this report also addresses issues like environmental impact assessment, framework environmental laws, regional cooperation and Afghanistan's participation in international environmental conventions.

UNEP field mission

In September 2002, a month-long UNEP mission comprising 20 Afghan and international scientists and experts visited 38 urban sites in four cities and 35 different rural locations.

During the UNEP field work a total of 60 samples were collected to test air, soil and water conditions and levels of chemical contamination. State-of-the-art satellite analyses also proved to be an invaluable tool, especially in areas not accessible due to security constraints. Through the use of Landsat satellite images, land-cover analysis could look back over a 25 year period to investigate wetland degradation, desertification and deforestation. Due to the security situation – ongoing conflict and dangers of mines and other unexploded ordinances – the UNEP mission was not able to cover all parts of Afghanistan. For example, safe access to the Ajar Valley or the cedar forests of Kunar and Nuristan provinces was not possible due to the ongoing local fighting.

UNEP partners and supporting organizations

Throughout the preparation of this assessment there has been full coordination with the Afghan Assistance Coordination Agency (AACA), and close cooperation with the Ministry of Irrigation, Water Resources and Environment, the Ministry of Public Health, and the Ministry of Agriculture and Animal Husbandry. Each of these ministries also seconded an experienced Afghan expert to the field mission.

UNEP team with Afghan guides investigating pistachio forests near Farkhar village

Post-Conflict Environmental Assessment

> **Sites visited by UNEP field teams**

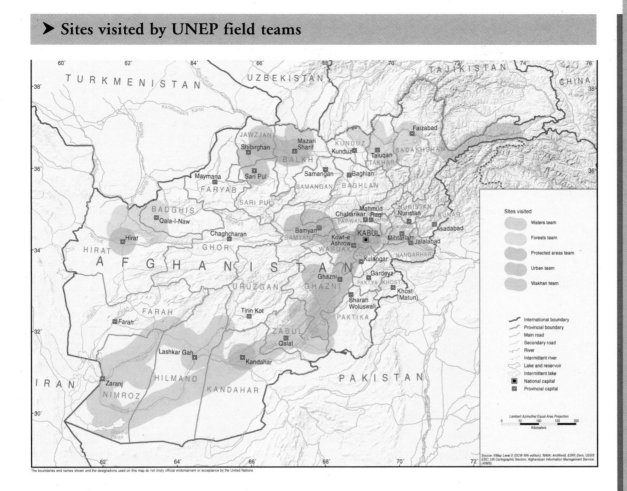

UNEP has been a member in the Natural Resources Management Programme Group in Kabul, a coordinating body that has been facilitated by the UN Food and Agriculture Organization (FAO). UNEP has also enjoyed good cooperation with the Asian Development Bank (ADB), and participated in an ADB-led mission on environment to Kabul in March 2002.

A number of non-governmental organizations (NGOs) in Afghanistan have also shared invaluable information with UNEP on the environmental situation of the country. They include the Agency for Rehabilitation and Energy Conservation in Afghanistan (AREA), the Afghan Relief Committee (ARC), Madera, and Save the Environment Afghanistan (SEA). Both ARC and SEA also generously seconded experts for the duration of the UNEP field assessment. Through difficult years, these committed organizations, and the entire Afghan NGO community, have been paving the way for sustainable development in the country.

The UNEP work in Afghanistan has been financially supported by the governments of Canada, Finland, Luxembourg and Switzerland. The close link between humanitarian and environmental needs in Afghanistan has been recognized in both the United Nations Immediate and Transitional Assistance Programme (ITAP) for Afghanistan in 2002 and in the Transitional Assistance Programme for Afghanistan (TAPA) in 2003.

Environmental experts were also seconded to participate in the UNEP mission by FAO, the United Nations Development Programme (UNDP), and the United Nations Economic Commission for Europe (UN-ECE). UNEP also had close cooperation with the United Nations Educational, Scientific and Cultural Organization (UNESCO), which carried out a special water mission to Afghanistan with one expert from UNEP. The United Nations Office for

Project Services (UNOPS) provided operational support for the field missions, including contracts, transport and communications equipment, while the United Nations Assistance Mission to Afghanistan (UNAMA) provided overall support and security. Good cooperation was also achieved with the United Nations Office for the Coordination of Humanitarian Affairs (OCHA), including the Joint UNEP-OCHA Environment Unit. Invaluable technical assistance was provided throughout the assessment by UNOSAT, the Afghanistan Information Management Service (AIMS), the UNEP World Conservation Monitoring Centre and by the UNEP Global Resource Information Database (GRID-Geneva).

Finally, international NGOs, including the World Conservation Union (IUCN), the International Institute for Sustainable Development (IISD), Green Cross International (GCI), the International Council for Game and Wildlife Conservation (CIC) and WWF – The Conservation Organization, have given their valuable support to the challenging work from the very beginning.

General findings and observations

In earlier post-conflict environmental assessments, UNEP has typically focused on war-related damage and environmental impacts from chemicals released from bombed targets. The picture in Afghanistan is different. The most serious issue in Afghanistan is the long-term environmental degradation caused, in part, by a complete collapse of local and national forms of governance.

Water is key to the health and well-being of Afghanistan's people, and essential to maintain agricultural productivity – the heart of the Afghan economy. However, both surface and groundwater resources have been severely affected by the drought, as well as by uncoordinated and unmanaged extraction. In many cases, deep wells have been drilled without considering the long-term impacts on regional groundwater resources, including traditional *karez* systems (underground water canals). Water resources across the country are also threatened by contamination from waste dumps, chemicals and open sewers. Many of the country's wetlands are completely dry and no longer support wildlife populations or provide

MARTYN MURRAY/UNEP, 2002

Restoration of the green cover and vegetation is a high priority to combat erosion, desertification and flood risks

Post-Conflict Environmental Assessment

ANTHONY FITZHERBERT/FAO, 2002

The Shrine of Ali in Mazar-e-Sharif is a symbol of Afghanistan's rich and diverse cultural history

agricultural inputs. For example, UNEP found that over 99 per cent of the Sistan wetland, a critically important haven for waterfowl, was completely dry. Furthermore, wind-blown sediments were in-filling irrigation canals and reservoirs, as well as covering roads, fields and villages, with an overall effect of increasing local vulnerability to drought. Improved water resource management will, in many regions, be an essential first step in rebuilding rural communities and improving human health. Maintaining water quality and quantity should be the overriding goal of all land-use planning activities and integrated water basin planning should be implemented across the country.

The forests and woodlands of Afghanistan supply important sources of fuelwood and construction materials critical for cooking, shelter and overall survival. Some trees, such as pistachio and almond, also supply sources of nuts that can supplement diets and generate modest incomes. Sadly, illegal harvesting is depleting forests and woodland resources, and widespread grazing is preventing regeneration. UNEP's satellite analyses revealed that conifer forests in the provinces of Nangarhar, Kunar and Nuristan have been reduced by an average of 50 per cent since 1978. Similarly, pistachio woodlands in the provinces of Badghis and Takhar were found to be highly degraded. With the loss of forests and vegetation, and excessive grazing and dry land cultivation, soils are being exposed to serious erosion from wind and rain. The productivity of the land base is declining, driving people from rural to urban areas in search of food and employment. Riverbanks are also eroding with the loss of stabilizing vegetation, and flood risks are increasing. Restoration of forests and other vegetation cover combined with grazing management are high priorities to combat erosion, desertification and flood risks.

In the urban environment, human health is being placed at risk by poor waste management practices and lack of proper sanitation. Hospitals are significant 'hotspots' as medical wastes are disposed of improperly. There are no proper landfills in any of the towns and cities, and none of the dumpsites are taking measures to prevent groundwater contamination or toxic air pollution from burning wastes. In some cases, such as in Herat, dumpsites

AFGHANISTAN

have been located in dry riverbeds upstream from the city. The first period of sustained rainfall could wash the dump's contents back down into the city centre. Proper management of sewage and wastes is clearly an urgent priority to protect human health.

UNEP also found evidence of a few polluting industrial activities operating without regard for environmental protection or the health of workers. These findings are especially alarming in observed cases where workers, including children, are exposed to chemical pollution.

Finally, the natural wildlife heritage of the country is also under threat. Flamingos have not bred successfully in Afghanistan for four years, and the last Siberian crane was seen in 1986. While the Wakhan Corridor contains healthy populations of endangered snow leopards and other mammals including Marco Polo sheep, active hunting is occurring in many regions of the country, either for sport, for meat, or in order to supply furs for sale to foreigners in Kabul. The legal status of all protected areas is currently in question, and no management is taking place to protect and conserve their ecological integrity and wildlife. Furthermore, less than 1 per cent of the land base is contained within protected areas – none of which cover the dwindling conifer forests of the east. One positive finding was that Band-e-Amir National Park, one of the most beautiful landscapes in all of Afghanistan, is in good hydrological condition despite the recent drought. This natural treasure has all of the characteristics of a World Heritage Site, and could become an important destination for nature tourism with proper management and community support.

Responsibility for implementing the recommendations contained in this report lies with the people of Afghanistan and their government institutions. The newly established Ministry of Irrigation, Water Resources and Environment must play a critical role in planning and preparing new laws, standards and activities to address the environmental management, protection and rehabilitation needs of the country. This should occur in full cooperation with the key sector ministries responsible for implementation, including Agriculture and Animal Husbandry, Public Health, Rural Development, Urban Development and Housing, Water and Power, and Mines and Industry. Mechanisms for planning, environmental education, public participation and enforcement must be developed between the various sector ministries and their partners at the central, regional and local levels.

It is important also to recognize that long-term improvements in the environmental conditions of the country cannot be achieved without sustained technical and financial assistance

The immense Buddhas of Bamiyan were destroyed in 2001

KOEN TOONEN/UNEP, 2002

CHARUDUTT MISHRA/UNEP, 2002

Boy with lambs in Raish Kaigar

from the international community. As part of this assessment, a thorough analysis was made on how Afghanistan could benefit from becoming an active partner in various multi-lateral environmental agreements, in particular the clean development mechanism of the Kyoto Protocol. Many of the solutions, like river basin management and control of the illegal timber trade, will also require improved regional, cross-border cooperation.

In Afghanistan, improving local livelihoods is strongly dependent on environmental protection and sustainable management of natural resources. While the environmental challenges facing Afghanistan are enormous, the will and the knowledge necessary to meet these challenges exists across the country. UNEP was extremely impressed by the highly skilled Afghans met during the mission, and by the resilience demonstrated by the Afghan people in the face of hardship. In many sites, despite tremendous material and financial handicaps, people were knowledgeable and dedicated to improving the environment. With support from the international community in the months ahead, Afghanistan can make great progress toward protecting its environment and achieving a form of development that will endure for generations to come.

Pekka Haavisto
Chairman
UNEP Afghanistan Task Force

AFGHANISTAN

Country context

Afghanistan is a land-locked country of plains and mountains. Below the high Khojak Pass on the country's southern border lies the Southwestern Plateau. This flat and harsh landscape is crossed by the Helmand River that feeds the marshes and lagoons of the Sistan basin. Rising from the plains are the Hindu Kush highlands, a central mountainous core, beyond which lie the Northern Plains.

Although elevation and aridity frequently combine to make dramatic landscapes, in a country that is almost entirely agrarian these same conditions make subsistence a constant challenge, and the livelihood of most people in Afghanistan is acutely vulnerable to climatic variation. The routine hardships faced by many rural Afghans have helped shape the attributes of resilience and independence for which the country is famous.

Scenic view at the confluence of the Wakhan and Pamir rivers

Extracting a living from the mountainous dry lands of Afghanistan has never been easy, but nearly 25 years of armed conflict, and four years of extreme drought, have created widespread human suffering and environmental devastation across the country. Warfare, lawlessness and food insecurity have made refugees of some four million Afghans – the equivalent to a quarter of the total country population at the time of the Soviet occupation in 1979. Infrastructure has been destroyed and many institutions and administrative systems have collapsed. The country is perhaps the most heavily mined in the world and large areas cannot be entered without risk. The nation's biological resources are being rapidly degraded by uncontrolled grazing, cultivation, water extraction, hunting and deforestation.

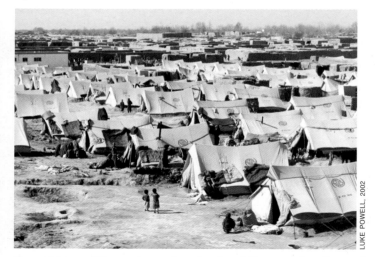

Drought conditions drove hundreds of thousands of people into temporary camps

Putting the country back on a path towards sustainable development will be an immense task, requiring long-term support from the international community. With careful planning, there remains potential to overcome the current problems and to rebuild institutional capacity and restore the natural resources of the country. However, no time should be wasted in seizing the opportunity to integrate environment into the reconstruction process for the current and future benefit of all Afghans.

A mined riverbed
en route to Farkhar
village

DAVID JENSEN/UNEP, 2002

Livelihoods

Afghanistan is an essentially agrarian country, with around 80 per cent of the population involved in farming or herding, or both. Two basic farming patterns exist: a mixed crop and livestock system, and the Kuchi pastoral system. The latter implies a nomadic existence, named after the Kuchi communities who undertake a seasonal transfer of grazing animals to different pastures (a practice termed transhumance).

Only a relatively small part of the land area of Afghanistan is suitable for arable farming or horticulture, including both irrigated as well as rain-fed farming. Prior to the Soviet occupation it is estimated that 85 per cent of the population derived their main livelihood from arable farming, horticulture and livestock husbandry, commonly in combination. More than half of all irrigated arable land lies north of the main Hindu Kush range in the drainage systems of the Amu Darya River. Much of the remaining irrigated land lies in the river basins draining southwest, west and southeast out from the central massif, most signifi-

cantly the basin of the Helmand River system. Although estimates vary, a recent source[1] suggests about 3.3 million ha (5 per cent of the total land area) is irrigated and regularly cropped, while 4.5 million ha (7 per cent) is rain-fed and is cropped opportunistically, depending on precipitation. Most of the rain-fed land lies in a 900-km long belt lying west to east along the northern foothills and plains. Increasing rural population pressure on available land over the last two to three generations has led to more and more traditional grazing land being

ANTHONY FITZHERBERT/UNEP, 2002

**Threshing wheat in the
Wakhan valley**

Irrigated area near Kunduz

cultivated for rain-fed wheat crops, even on very steep slopes and in the highest mountains. Yields have proved to be uncertain and crop failures common. The environmental degradation resulting from the destruction of the original ground cover and consequent erosion is widespread and very serious. Of the remaining area, about half (57 million ha according to some estimates) is rangeland and open *Artimesia* steppe used for extensive livestock grazing, the rest having little or no vegetative ground cover.

Wheat is the main crop cultivated on both irrigated and rain-fed land throughout the country, reflecting Afghanistan's cultural dependence on bread as the staple diet. On average, per capital consumption of wheat is 167 kg per year. Barley is cultivated at the highest altitudes for grain and at lower altitudes as green fodder. However, cropping and rotational systems show considerable regional variations depending on climate, precipitation, the availability of irrigation water and altitude. For example, below 1 500 metres (m) of altitude, double cropping is common on irrigated land where there is sufficient water. Wheat is sown in the autumn and early winter, followed where possible by a second summer crop of rice, maize or

Terraced fields west of Mazar-e-Sharif

Post-Conflict Environmental Assessment

pulses, depending on location. Above 1 500 m only single cropping is possible even on irrigated land. At higher altitudes (over 2 000 m) most of the irrigated crop is sown in the spring. Rather sophisticated traditional crop rotations are practised in many places, including a combination of cereal crops with a variety of pulses and fodder crops such as annual clover (*Trifolium* spp) and perennial alfalfa (*Medicaga sativa*). A wide variety of vegetables including onions and potatoes are cultivated both for subsistence and as commercial crops. Potatoes are particularly significant in the Bamiyan, Maidan and Jalalabad regions. The quality and flavour of Afghan melons of many varieties have been noted for centuries, and large quantities are exported to neighbouring countries such as Pakistan.

Other high-value crops such as cumin, sesame, linseed and sugar cane are cultivated where appropriate. Cotton is still grown in some provinces, such as Helmand, Baghlan and Kunduz. Other industrial crops such as sugar beet are no longer cultivated following the collapse of the industries that sustained them.

Afghanistan has also long been noted for many kinds of fruit (including apricots, apples, pomegranates, and grapes) and nuts (principally almonds, walnuts and wild pistachio). Such crops can provide twenty times more than wheat from the equivalent area. In the 1970s dried fruit, raisins and nuts contributed more than 40 per cent of the country's foreign exchange earnings, although the years of conflict have meant that the country has lost some of its former market niches. The rapid expansion of orchard plantations and the adoption of modern systems and varieties occurred between 1989 and 1999. This trend has been very much slowed down by the drought.

Poppy field in Kunar province

In recent years Afghanistan has earned notoriety as the world's largest producer of opium, contributing some 75 per cent of the global illegal supply[2]. The opium poppy has been cultivated for many centuries in Afghanistan, but the period of conflict has led to a massive expansion in production. In the southwest and eastern provinces, in particular Helmand, Kandahar, Uruzghan, Nangarhar, Laghman and Kunar, opium poppy has increasingly replaced wheat as the most significant autumn-sown cash crop and as a spring-sown crop in Badakhshan province. In 1999 output was estimated by the United Nations Office on Drugs and Crime (UNODC) at about 4 600 tonnes of opium gum from a total area of 91 000 ha. This fell to 3 300 tonnes from 81 000 ha in 2000[3] largely because of the drought and more dramatically to 185 tonnes from 8 000 ha in 2001 due to a strictly enforced ban imposed by the Taliban government[4]. The departure of the Taliban saw a return to massive poppy cultivation in 2002, which UNODC estimates at about 3 400 tonnes from 74 000 ha[5]. The farm gate price of opium gum has risen dramatically from about US$30 per kg in 2000 to its current level of about US$350–US$400 per kg in late 2002. Wheat is the main seasonal competitor crop for opium poppy. However, while it is estimated that a 2.5 tonne per hectare crop of wheat might earn a farmer US$440, the equivalent land sown to poppy will earn him US$18 400[6]. This makes opium an almost irresistible crop for rural families struggling to rebuild their lives and improve their livelihoods. It is hardly a surprise to find that 2002 also saw the spread of poppy cultivation into a number of provinces and districts where it had not been cultivated previously.

Wheat straw along with other crop residues, wild plants and weeds and fodder crops such as lucerne, clover and vetches help to sustain livestock, especially through the winter months. Cattle and sheep provide milk, meat, wool and hides, as well as dung for fuel. Oxen are the main source of power for cultivation, while horses and donkeys provide rural transportation. Most rural families keep a cow or two for milk, and certain local breeds, such as the Kandahari and Kunari, are well recognised. There is evidence of cross-breeding with western breeds in many locations. Not all rural families keep sheep and goats but flocks are found in most villages, sometimes running into hundreds. Several different, distinct local breeds of sheep are recognised, mostly of the fat-tailed/fat-rumped type. Although animal traction is still common throughout Afghanistan, some areas in northern Afghanistan and in the southwest in the Helmand/Arghandab basins are now highly mechanized due to larger land holdings and irrigation. In the southwest in particular, incomes earned from opium cultivation and comparatively

ANTHONY FITZHERBERT/UNEP, 2002

Grazing livestock in Yupgaz valley

large land holdings have led to a rapid increase in agricultural mechanization in recent years, helped by a flourishing import market of affordable Iranian tractors.

In 1978-79[7] sheep numbers were estimated to be about 14 million and goat numbers at 3 million. Numbers fell dramatically during the ten years of Soviet war, according to some estimates by as much as 40 per cent. In the ten years after 1989, a period of comparative rural peace and good grazing, sheep numbers rose to an estimated 24 million and goat numbers to 9 million by 1999[8]. Persistent drought and poor grazing since 1999 has led to a massive reduction in flock numbers (possibly by as much as 70 per cent[9]) and many *kuchi* families who have lost all their livestock have been forced to become refugees or move into camps for internally displaced people (IDPs) close to feeding centres. Distress selling at below market value is thought to have been widespread. It is hoped that the better grazing conditions in 2002 will have helped the start of a recovery, and there is some anecdotal evidence that lambing averages were well up on previous years.

The nomadic/transhumant Kuchis are mainly ethnic Pashtun. Collectively they own about one-third of the national flock. Typically flocks are comprised of 80 per cent sheep and 20 per cent goats[10], with horses, donkeys and camels used for transport and their traditional homes being black goat-hair tents. Typically, many of the Pashtun Kuchis winter in Pakistan

Post-Conflict Environmental Assessment

Kuchi tents near Qala-i-Nau

as far south as the southern Punjab and the Sind, moving back to Afghanistan in the spring and gradually into the high mountains to 3 000 m altitude and above in the summer as the snow recedes. Other smaller groups of professional herders also exist, such as the felt yurt-dwelling Kyrgyz in the Pamir who herd yaks as well as sheep, goats and camels, and the Gujar cattle owners who winter in the Punjab and North West Frontier of Pakistan and summer in upper Kunar and other border Afghan provinces.

Traditional migration routes have often been seriously disrupted in the recent years of conflict, as for instance across the Taliban/Northern Alliance front line in Takhar. Ethnic and religious antagonism between the Pashtun Kuchis and the local resident Hazaras and Aimaq in the central Hindu Kush massif has led to an ebb and flow of *kuchi* access to the Hazarajat. At present the retreat of the Taliban, who gave military support to the Pashtun Kuchis, means that access to the central mountains is not encouraged by the local Hazaras, who own their own resident flocks and herds.

Small-scale industries exist in Kabul and other centres, primarily producing goods for domestic consumption. Natural gas has been a valuable export commodity in the past, followed by dried fruit and nuts, fresh fruit, karakul (sheep) skins and raw cotton. The potential exists for further exploitation of mineral deposits and semi-precious stones. There is currently a major illegal trade in cedar timber, mainly with Pakistan.

People

Afghanistan is culturally highly diverse, with around 20 distinct ethnic groups. Some groups tend to occupy particular areas of the country, while others are more scattered, or mainly urban. Traditional tribal rivalries are an important factor in social relationships, and the diversity of ethnic groups is reflected in the current composition of the Transitional Authority. The two principal languages are Pashto (the language of the Pashtuns) and Dari (a variant of Persian). Afghanistan is a Muslim country, with the majority Sunni and most of the remainder Shi'a.

Pashtuns make up the largest single ethnic group. Living mainly in the wide belt of land south of the Hindu Kush, Pashtuns have, since the 18th century, tended to be the dominant element in national governance. Four other groups – the Turkoman, Uzbek, Tajik and Kyrgyz – extend into northern Afghanistan from parts of Central Asia. Of these, the Tajiks

2

FROM TOP: LEFT TO RIGHT: ANTHONY FITZHERBERT, DENNIS FENTON, KOEN TOONEN, DAVID JENSEN, MARTYN MURRAY, CHARUDUTT MISHRA, DAVID JENSEN, RENE NIJENHUIS, PETER ZAHLER, CHARUDUTT MISHRA/UNEP, 2002

Faces of Afghanistan

form the second largest group in the country. The Hazara and Aimaq people live mainly in the mountainous centre, with Baluch and Brahui people in the dry lands of the southwest. Of the many smaller communities, the Nuristani and Pasha'i in the northeastern Nuristan province are particularly distinct culturally and linguistically, and were only converted to Islam in the 19th century.

Despite the considerable loss of life and forced migration during the recent years of conflict, available estimates suggest that the country's total population has risen fairly steadily from more than 8 million in 1950 to nearly 22 million in 2000[11]. An estimated 4 million Afghans resided outside the country in early 2002. However, by December 2002, around 1.8 million had returned following the downfall of the Taliban government[12]. Almost 50 per cent of all returnees have resettled in the central region, while the eastern, northern, southern and western regions have received 22, 21, 6 and 3 per cent respectively[13].

Post-Conflict Environmental Assessment

In 1950 an estimated 94 per cent of the population dwelt in rural areas. By 2000 this figure had fallen to 78 per cent, with urban populations rising largely in response to drought and conflict[14]. The country is divided into 32 provinces, with Kabul as the largest city and the administrative capital.

Maternal mortality has recently been estimated at around 1 600 deaths per 100 000 live births[15]. Among children, one in four do not survive beyond five years[16]. Both rates are among the highest in the world. Over 200 000 women have been made widows by the war[17]. Female-headed households comprise the majority of those under the poverty level of US$1 a day. The Taliban pursued a policy of extreme discrimination against women and girls. In 1999 illiteracy among women was 80 per cent compared with 50 per cent for men. In 1998 girls accounted for 32 per cent of primary enrolment and 25 per cent of secondary enrolment[17].

Topography

Afghanistan's total land area approaches 650 000 km². Most of the land (some 63 per cent) is mountainous, using formal criteria based on slope and elevation, and more than a quarter (27 per cent) lies above 2 500 m[19]. Rising to about 5 100 m, the rugged Hindu Kush range, covering 456 000 km², forms the central core of the country from where ridges fan out to the west and south, with the Paropamisus mountains extending westwards to the border with Iran. The Hindu Kush peaks rise even further in elevation toward northeast Afghanistan, to around 7 000 m in the high-altitude Wakhan Corridor, where the Pamir and Karakoram mountains meet. This corridor extends as a narrow strip of land to a short border with China, separating Tajikistan from Pakistan.

The doorstep of the Hindu Kush

The most extensive flatlands are located in the southwest of the country, centred

Rock formation rising from the arid flatlands around Delaram

around the internal drainage basin of the Helmand River, and in the north of the country, between the northern foothills of the Hindu Kush and the Amu Darya (Oxus) River (here marking the border with Tajikistan and Uzbekistan). Both regions, the southwest in particular, include large areas of sand desert.

Climate

The climate is continental in nature, with cold winters and hot summers. Most of the country is semi-arid or arid, with low amounts of precipitation and high or very high variability between years. Snowfall is concentrated in the central mountains and the higher ranges of the northeast. Winter temperatures are extremely low in both these areas, below -15°C for many weeks during winter. Most of Afghanistan is influenced by weather fronts from the Mediterra-

Semi-arid landscape near Bamiyan

LUKE POWELL, 2002

nean, with low and erratic rainfall, typically in spring. The east of the country lies near the margin of the monsoon system affecting the Indian subcontinent. Here, parts of the eastern provinces, including Kunar, Nuristan, Laghman, and Nangarhar, have up to 1 200 mm of rainfall in summer (roughly five times the national average).

Rivers, lakes and wetlands

Five principal drainage regions can be distinguished, with the Koh-e-Baba mountain range in the geographic centre of the country as the primary watershed. With one exception, all drainage systems in Afghanistan end in closed internal basins.

The major river is the Amu Darya, which rises in the Pamirs, forms much of the northern border of Afghanistan, and traverses a large area of Central Asia, drying up before it reaches the Aral Sea. The Murghab and the Hari-Rud both drain the northwest sector of the Hindu Kush, flowing west then north to terminate in southern Turkmenistan, where they contribute to groundwater resources. The Helmand, which collects rain and snow-melt from the

View of the Amu Darya River near Kalaktal village

DAVID JENSEN/UNEP, 2002

Post-Conflict Environmental Assessment

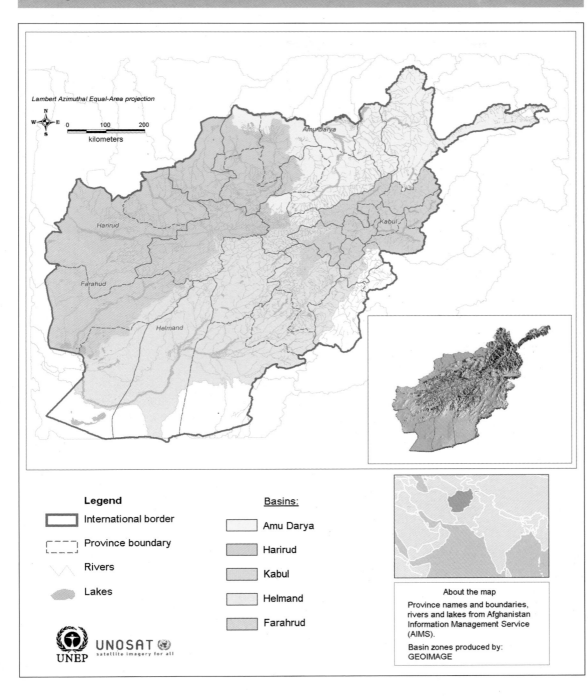

Lambert Azimuthal Equal-Area projection

0   100   200
kilometers

Amu Darya

Harirud

Kabul

Farahud

Helmand

Legend

▭ International border

▭ Province boundary

Rivers

Lakes

UNEP   UNOSAT
         satellite imagery for all

Basins:

Amu Darya

Harirud

Kabul

Helmand

Farahrud

About the map

Province names and boundaries, rivers and lakes from Afghanistan Information Management Service (AIMS).

Basin zones produced by: GEOIMAGE

southern slopes of the Hindu Kush, is the longest river entirely within Afghanistan, its catchment extending over some 31 per cent of the country. Helmand waters flow through the arid southwest plains to enter the marshlands and lakes of the Sistan basin, which is shared with Iran. The Kabul River system, which drains around 9 per cent of the country around the capital, traverses the Jalalabad Gorge to join the Indus River in Pakistan.

With the exception of the Amu Darya, which receives inputs from countries to the north, most rivers in Afghanistan – and almost the entire supply of the country's water for irrigation, drinking, and maintenance of wetland ecosystems – are derived from rainfall within the country's own borders and the seasonal melting of snow and permanent ice-fields in the mountains. The persistence of snow and ice are closely related to prevailing temperature, so this source of water is likely to be at risk from continuing global warming. In general, the peak flow of melt-water occurs in springtime, and flow is sporadic or non-existent in many watercourses during the summer. In years with heavy precipitation, rapid runoff can cause flooding and mudslides in the spring.

There are very few lakes and marshland areas. Because of their rarity, existing wetlands are particularly valuable for people as sources of water and other resources such as reeds, and as habitat for wetland species, notably for breeding and migrant waterbirds. The largest permanent lakes are those at Band-e-Amir in the central highlands, and at high altitudes in the Wakhan Corridor. Other lakes are more variable in extent. By far the largest lie within the Sistan basin, where lakes and flooded marshland cover up to 4 000 km^2 in times of good water supply (occasionally, even these have been known to shrink or dry completely). As almost half of the Sistan wetlands lie in Iran, transboundary management of this resource is required. Other important wetland areas include Dasht-e-Nawar, Ab-e-Estada and Kole Hashmat Khan.

Land cover and biodiversity

Afghanistan has a wide range of ecosystems, including glaciers and high-alpine vegetation (particularly in the extreme northeast, including the Wakhan Corridor), montane coniferous and mixed forest, open dry woodland with juniper, pistachio or almond, semi-desert scrub, sand and stony deserts, rivers, lakes and marshland. The more closed types of mixed and coniferous forests occur mainly in the east, along the

ANTHONY FITZHERBERT/UNEP, 2002

Pin cushion thorns, high-alpine vegetation

AGENCY FOR REHABILITATION, ENVIRONMENT AND ENERGY CONSERVATION (AREA), 2002

Conifer forests of Kunar province

border with Pakistan, where precipitation tends to be more regular and abundant. Areas of open woodland remain mainly on the northern slopes of the Hindu Kush.

Vegetation cover in Afghanistan has been modified significantly through millennia of human occupation. Most of the country appears to be subject to some degree of land degradation. Much of the land surface is used as rangeland for grazing livestock. Tree cover was formerly more extensive than at present.

The potential for regrowth is likely to be seriously affected by heavy fuelwood collection or timber harvesting that far outstrips woodland regeneration, and by browsing and grazing domestic livestock. FAO reported that even during the 1970s "the few remaining forest areas of the country are being destroyed at an alarming rate"[20]. Soil erosion is also a serious problem due to the loss of protective vegetation cover.

➤ **Afghanistan land cover, 2002**

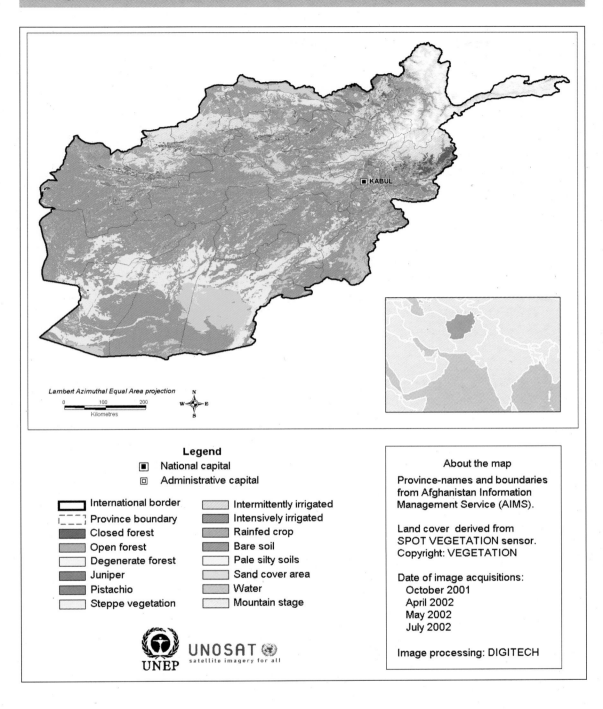

As witnessed by the many observations recorded in the memoirs of Babur, the founder of the Mughal dynasty who ruled Afghanistan from 1483 to 1530, the country was renowned for its rich wildlife. Some species then present, such as tiger, cheetah and wild ass, have disappeared from the country. However, with its diversity of different habitats, Afghanistan retains a wide variety of fauna.

Many of the larger mammals in Afghanistan are categorized by the World Conservation Union (IUCN) as globally threatened[21]. These include snow leopard (*Uncia uncia*), wild goat (*Capra aegagrus*), markhor (*Capra falconeri*), Marco Polo sheep (*Ovis ammon polii*), urial (*Ovis orientalis*), and Asiatic black bear (*Ursus thibetanus*). Other mammals of interest include ibex (*Capra ibex*), wolf (*Canis lupus*), red fox (*Vulpes vulpes*), jackal (*Canis aureus*), caracal (*Caracal*

The globally threatened markhor (Capra falconeri) is among Afghanistan's large mammals

BRENT HUFFMAN/ULTIMATEUNGULATE

caracal), manul or Pallas's cat (*Otocolobus manul*), striped hyena (*Hyena hyena*), rhesus macaque (*Macaca mulatta*), and brown bear (*Ursus arctos*).

Many of Afghanistan's bird species are also globally threatened, including the Siberian crane (*Grus leucogeranus*), white-headed duck (*Oxyura leucocephala*), marbled teal (*Marmaronetta angustirostris*), Pallas's sea-eagle (*Haliaeetus leucoryphus*), greater spotted eagle (*Aquilla clanga*), imperial eagle (*Aquilla heliaca*), lesser kestrel (*Falco naumanni*), corncrake (*Crex crex*), sociable lapwing (*Vanellus gregaria*) and the pale-backed pigeon (*Columba hodgsonii*). Among these, the Siberian crane is of particular significance. This species is categorized by IUCN as Critically Endangered and is believed to face an extremely high risk of extinction in the wild in the immediate future. The global population, estimated to contain 2 500–3 000 birds, is divided into three groups[21]. Only a single breeding pair may remain in the central group, which formerly used wetlands in Afghanistan (and Iran) as stopover points during migration between breeding grounds in Russia and the main wintering area in India[22]. Ab-e-Estada was the key resting site in Afghanistan.

Other birds of interest found in Afghanistan include greater flamingo (*Phoenicopterus ruber)* and houbara bustard (*Chlamydotis undulata*).

The country has one endemic bird species, Meinertzhagen's snow finch *(Montifringila theresae)*, and major breeding populations of six other restricted regional species: yellow-eyed pigeon *(Columba eversmanni)*, plain willow warbler *(Phylloscopus neglectus)*, Brooks's willow warbler *(P. subviridis)*, variable wheatear *(Oenanthe picata)* and Dead Sea sparrow *(Passer moabiticus)*. The population of yellow-eyed pigeon is particularly important because the species is rare and declining throughout its Central Asian range. Afghanistan also has significant numbers of breeding lammergeier (*Gypaetus barbatus*), black vulture (*Aegypius monachus*) and other birds of prey.

Among reptiles, four species are believed to be restricted to Afghanistan: the geckos *Asiocolotes levitoni* and *Cyrtopodion voraginosus*, and the lacertid lizards *Eremias afghanistanica* and *E. aria*. The salamander *Batrachuperus mustersi* occurs only in mountain streams in the central Hindu Kush of Afghanistan and is believed to be at risk from habitat modification and conflict.

The freshwater fishes of Afghanistan have been little studied, but many are believed to be endemic. The Helmand River system in particular, lying almost entirely within the country, has up to three species of snow trout *Schizothorax* and five loaches *Noemachilus* that appear to be restricted to Afghanistan (species taxonomy in both genera is not well established).

Post-Conflict Environmental Assessment

Diversity at the genetic level is not fully known, but with the region's long history of subsistence farming and crop improvements, there is thought to be major diversity in genetic resources for food and agriculture. Local wheat varieties remain important, particularly in regions with a wide range of topographic and climatic conditions, such as in the Hazarajat (central mountains), and have been of particular value for rain-fed cropping during the recent drought. More generally, particularly in irrigated land, these have been rapidly replaced by improved varieties, exchanging benefits such as winter hardiness for the increased risks of genetic uniformity. Regional varieties of cereal and other crops have been little-studied to date, and the same is true of the many trees – including species of pistachio, almond, walnut, apricot and others – that provide harvests of nuts and fruit. Among wild plants and animals, a number of species reach their eastern or western limits in Afghanistan, and the region may thus provide a source of high intraspecies genetic diversity from outlier populations at the edge of their ranges.

Ab-e-Estada provided important migratory habitat for the critically endangered Siberian crane (*Grus leucogeranus*)

GEORGE ARCHIBALD/INTERNATIONAL CRANE FOUNDATION

Urban environment

3

Introduction

High levels of unemployment, a failing electricity supply network and assorted public health problems are having a profound effect on the quality of urban life in Afghanistan. These problems are compounded by the increasing numbers of people who are moving into urban areas to escape rural hardships and insecurity arising from degraded environments and loss of livelihoods. Returning refugees further increase the pressure on urban infrastructure and resources. Approximately two million refugees returned to Afghanistan in 2002[24], with more than half a million returning to Kabul alone. Another 1.5 million are expected to return in 2003[25]. On the positive side, Afghanistan's economy is gradually recovering and foreign investment is on the rise. The period ahead offers a crucial opportunity to integrate environmental management solutions into its social and economic strategies so that peace, growth and increased prosperity can be ensured for the long term.

The objective of UNEP's urban assessment was to survey the environmental conditions in major population centres and to recommend priority

Marketplace in Mazar-e-Sharif

SØREN HVILSHØJ/UNEP, 2002

actions for the Afghan government and its international partners. UNEP's principal aim was to identify threats to human health and the environment, and obstacles to the sustainable development of Afghanistan's economy.

UNEP visited four cities between 8 and 29 September 2002 – Herat, Kabul, Kandahar and Mazar-e-Sharif – focusing on five environmental aspects: solid waste, wastewater, water supply, public facilities and industrial sites and, to a lesser extent, air pollution.

In each of the cities UNEP interviewed key stakeholders, including government officials, community leaders, non-governmental organizations (NGOs), citizens and international agency staff. Assessments were made of relevant environmental policies and practices, samples were collected, and relationships between the different sectors examined. Cross-cutting issues such as land use, worker health and safety, employment and environmental awareness were also considered. Lastly, possible environmental management options for each sector or site were identified.

Within the four cities visited, UNEP chose sites for inspection and analysis based on a preliminary survey of the cities' environmental infrastructure and resources, as well as information on former and current industrial sites. The environmental information available to UNEP was extremely limited and often outdated. Many records were destroyed during the period of conflict, and in many cases data have never been collected systematically. As a result, information provided verbally by city officials and members of the public formed an important part of background data. The lack of available environmental information reflects the larger problem of institutional capacity in the environmental sector, an issue discussed more fully in Chapter 5.

A number of air, soil and water samples were also collected by UNEP in order to obtain new data and make an independent scientific assessment of the prevailing conditions. Some time-sensitive water samples for measuring bacterial contamination were analysed in the field, while the remaining samples of water were analysed under certified laboratory conditions.

Principle findings and conclusions

■ Waste management

Despite low levels of consumption and production, weak management of solid waste is already one of the country's most glaring environmental problems. If rapid population growth, refugee returns and urbanization continue as predicted, the stresses on an already inadequate system will worsen.

In response to current needs, the international community has taken initial steps toward implementing waste management programmes. However, many of these initiatives will provide only short-term fixes to the problems, due to inadequate planning and little consideration of long-term environmental impacts. There is, therefore, an urgent need for Afghanistan to develop a set of comprehensive waste management policies that will address the entire life cycle of waste – from consumer behaviour to final disposal.

Key findings:

Waste composition: In general, solid waste loads are not being managed properly. Where collection facilities exist, hazardous, medical, industrial, household and inert (soil, gravel, stone and dust) wastes are mixed together without regard to safety considerations or collection efficiency. For example, UNEP found that over 50 per cent of the waste material is inert. This adds a tremendous amount of unnecessary material to the cities' landfills and increases transportation costs and vehicle emissions. In approximate terms, the remainder of the waste includes plastic (10 per cent), household waste (5 per cent) and assorted urban, industrial, and medical waste. Hazardous wastes form a small component, with unknown human health and environmental risks for both collection and storage. The screening of waste at transfer stations could dramatically reduce waste volumes, the area of landfill used, transport-related traffic and emissions, and, consequently, levels of environmental risk.

SCOTT CROSSETT/UNEP, 2002

Inert materials at Herat dumpsite

Collection: Waste collection efforts are far from uniform in Afghanistan's cities. In some areas of Kabul,

Waste collector at Kandahar

SØREN HVILSHØJ/UNEP, 2002

Districts 5 and 6 for example, waste is piling up in the community's narrow streets and is being contaminated by human excrement from the open sewer. Due to a lack of adequate incineration facilities at Kabul hospital, medical wastes are also improperly disposed of on city streets. This is putting people at risk of exposure to bacteria, viruses, toxic materials and other hazards. In Kandahar, by contrast, UN-Habitat and the municipality have established collection points for waste in each of the city's six districts. Waste collectors, paid by the project, collect waste from houses in wheelbarrows and take it to collection points where it is loaded into vehicles and transported to the city's Mian Koo landfill. In Herat, approximately 160–170 m³ of waste is collected daily from 182 waste collections points throughout the city.

Vehicles: The lack of proper waste collection vehicles is a common problem. Kabul's shortage of vehicles restricts regular waste collection from the city centre and a few other districts. With UN-Habitat's assistance, Kabul may be moving toward a waste management model involving public-private partnerships that could potentially alleviate the vehicle resource problem. Kandahar, by contrast, has small, 1-2 ton vehicles, necessitating many more trips than a normal-sized truck would make. In addition, most of the waste load is inert material, with the result that fuel is wasted and the vehicles are being used more than is necessary, with resultant wear, higher maintenance costs and shorter life span.

Dumpsite selection: Afghanistan has no proper sanitary landfills, and is currently relying on unmanaged dumpsites for waste storage. The absence of appropriate dumpsite selection processes, including environmental risk assessments, is a significant problem in Afghanistan. For example, the siting of Kandahar's Mian Koo dumpsite in a dry river valley on the side of a mountain above the city is completely inappropriate. Heavy rains will almost certainly send hundreds, if not thousands of tonnes of waste back into the city via the river system. A similar situation exists at Herat's Qamar Qalla landfill where waste is spread over a large gravel area in a dried-out riverbed in a mountain valley above the city. The first period of sustained rainfall could wash the dump's contents back down into Herat. In Kabul, the Kampani dumpsite is located upstream and extremely close to a drinking water well field that may soon be expanded in order to meet the city's growing demand for water. The potential for cross-contamination of the water supply is significant. Mazar-e-Sharif, by contrast, could provide a model for the rest of Afghanistan: located within a reasonable distance from the town centre, a recycling/transfer station could be located nearby, and a shallow-depth landfill constructed on site. At the same time, it is distant enough from the town as not to present a problem to the urban community.

Waste management: In addition to often being sited inappropriately, UNEP found that Afghanistan's landfills are not being managed properly. The groundwater system that feeds wells near Kabul's Kampani landfill, for example, is not protected from contamination due to toxic leachate. As a result, drinking water quality could easily be compromised. Similarly, the city's now inactive landfill, Cham-Tala, contains over 30 hectares of waste piled 2-3 m high. Although the site is relatively stable during the current drought, there is no gas or leachate monitoring or management system in place, and future rainfall could quickly cause instability and pollution. At Kandahar's Mian Koo landfill, the municipality has started to

Post-Conflict Environmental Assessment

SØREN HVILSHØJ/UNEP, 2002

Children collecting scrap materials at Qamar Qalla dumpsite, Herat

burn material to clear the site of potential wind-blown plastic litter without monitoring the toxic content of emissions. For Kandahar, which already experiences air pollution, the dioxins and furans released into the atmosphere from burning plastic are further endangering public health. In Herat, elderly men and children have free access to the landfill and are extracting plastic for recycling from waste that contains clinical and animal waste. The risks to health from this activity are compounded by the fact that the landfill is infested with flies that may well be carrying diseases.

Medical waste management: Afghanistan's medical waste is very poorly managed, posing a high and direct risk to human health and the environment. Waste from Herat Regional Hospital, for example, is treated like ordinary municipal waste – collected by municipal workers and carted to the city's unprotected landfill. Diseases, bacteria and viruses are very likely being spread through the air, and precious groundwater supplies are being contaminated. UNEP found similar situations in Mazar-e-Sharif and Kandahar. In many cases, medical wastes are being discarded into open streets and areas where public access is not controlled.

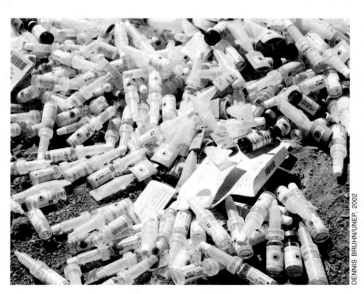

DENNIS BRUHN/UNEP, 2002

Medical waste at Kandahar dumpsite

AFGHANISTAN

Recycling/composting: There are positive developments emanating from UN-Habitat's efforts to promote the 'reduce, re-use, recycle' approach. Kandahar, for example, is planning to initiate recycling of plastics, cans, clothes, and paper - a project which is seeking to involve a local plastics factory and farmers. Mazar-e-Sharif's hopes to introduce composting at its landfill site. This would reduce waste for final disposal while creating a fertilizer-type product for farmers.

Health education: Health education initiatives are developing in Afghanistan's cities. For example, UN-Habitat is running a health education programme in partnership with the municipality of Kandahar and the Provincial Health Department as well as other national and international partners. The project is training 80 female health education workers to provide community outreach in Kandahar's six districts on subjects such as waste management, hygiene and health. The city will also participate in a joint initiative (with the TEAR Fund, a Christian relief and development organization) to broadcast health information over local radio stations.

■ Wastewater

The current level of sanitation in Afghanistan's urban areas is disturbingly poor. In 2000, it was estimated that only 8–12 per cent of the urban population had access to adequate sanitation. Wastewater collection barely exists in cities, often spewing into open gutters and canals – places where children gather to play. Treatment of wastewater, too, is nearly non-existent. Perhaps worst of all, urban drinking water supplies are being cross-contaminated with coliform bacteria (such as *Escherichia coli*, which infests the large intestine of both humans and animals) posing a considerable risk to public health. This finding was verified in water samples that UNEP took from municipal supply systems, private wells and hospital operating rooms in the cities it visited.

Key findings:

Open sewers: Open sewers carry wastewater that is highly contaminated with numerous pathogens, including *E. coli*. Direct exposure to pathogens is seriously jeopardizing public health. The risk is worst for children, some of whom are dying of cholera and other diseases resulting from poor water protection practices. On several occasions, UNEP witnessed sewer water being used to wash crops and for drinking. For example, Kabul Districts 5 and 6 have bad open sewers, and it is commonplace to see street traders washing food produce in the sewers before selling it to customers. After following shallow open ditches between houses to larger open troughs along main roads, the districts' sewer waters eventually flow into the Kabul River, the channel of which runs through many of the city's districts. Almost dry from drought, the river is clearly incapable of sustaining such heavy organic

Open sewer in District 5 of Kabul

SCOTT CROSSETT/UNEP, 2002

Post-Conflict Environmental Assessment

SCOTT CROSSETT/UNEP, 2002

Children playing in effluent stream in Herat

loading. Worse, the river is used for drinking water and for washing clothes. This is a common scenario throughout Afghanistan's cities.

Cross-contamination of water supplies: Water samples taken in Kabul Districts 5 and 6 clearly indicate that the city's drinking water quality is cross-contaminated by sewage. The samples revealed high levels (ranging from 18 to above 100 counts of bacteria in 100 ml of water) of contamination with coliform bacteria. According to the World Health Organisation (WHO), *no* levels of these pathogens are acceptable in 100-ml samples, the quantities tested by UNEP. This suggests that groundwater wells only 10–25 m deep throughout the city are at risk of contamination from surface sewers, damaged septic tanks and waste deposits. Some of this material contains medical waste, which can spread disease and viruses. When the current drought ends, cases of cross-contamination will very probably worsen, perhaps significantly, as rising groundwater levels wash out contaminants. The proper control of sewage is clearly an urgent priority.

Wastewater collection: There are a few notable exceptions to the open sewers described above. In Kabul Districts 9 and 16, for example, wastewater is being collected and treated. Kandahar is making plans for closed canalization. A 5.5-km section of Herat has stormwater drains and sewers. This section is expected to double in size under a current project supported by Germany. Unfortunately, this scheme discharges directly into the Carobar River. Furthermore, the existing sewer outfall is located approximately 500 m from the river due to decreased water levels from drought conditions. As a result, raw sewage flows openly past houses to the river. UNEP witnessed children playing in the effluent stream at its confluence with the river. The municipality of Herat has requested World Bank funding to build a sewage treatment plant adjacent to the sewage outfall.

Wastewater treatment: Only one city in Afghanistan collects wastewater and delivers it to a wastewater treatment plant: Kabul. This service is provided to two areas of the city (Districts 9 and 16) that are home to approximately 100 000 residents. The treatment plant processes about 12 000 m^3 of wastewater daily, discharging its effluent into the Kabul River.

Process sludge is dried and used for fertilizer. UNEP samples of the treated effluent, however, found bacteriological coliforms including *E. coli*. Despite these shortcomings, the plant provides an important starting point for reducing the pollution burden on the Kabul River, which is receiving direct sewage discharges throughout the city. Samples taken from the river revealed counts of over 100 of both *E. coli* and total coliform in 100 ml of water.

Wastewater treatment plant in Kabul

Septic tanks: Kandahar, like other cities in Afghanistan, lacks a sewer system and wastewater treatment plant. The city's preferred option for treatment is the septic tank system. Indeed, such systems are mandatory in all new buildings and are installed at a depth of 2 m. Private contractors empty the tanks, and the slurry is spread onto agricultural land outside the city limits. Prior to the drought the water table was only 3 m below the surface. Should the water table return to this historical level, there will be only a 1-m buffer zone separating the tanks from the groundwater. This creates the possibility of groundwater infiltration of the septic tanks should rains elevate the water levels. Nevertheless, well-maintained septic tanks provide a valuable interim solution to Kandahar's severe sanitation problems, and will reduce immediate risks to the city's environment and human health. In Herat, UN-Habitat is helping the city by building latrines that are connected to septic tanks. The contents of the tank are delivered to farms and discharged onto agricultural land. UN-Habitat is also replacing a number of Herat's soak-away ponds (open pits in which wastewater gradually filters into the ground layer) with sealed concrete septic tanks.

■ Water supply

Reliable access to a safe water supply, a fundamental need of any society, is virtually non-existent in Afghanistan's urban areas. UNEP's assessment clearly documents that city water supplies have been overwhelmed by wastewater infiltration and are ridden with *E. coli* and coliforms. These conditions represent a severe threat to public health that is likely to worsen as demographic pressures on Afghanistan's cities increase in the years ahead. While updated figures are not available, previous estimates concerning access to safe water range from 12 to 23 per cent of the urban population.

Key findings:

Groundwater management: There are two key problems concerning management of groundwater resources in Afghanistan's cities: a general lack of understanding about the underlying geologic conditions, and poor monitoring data of both supply and quality. For example, Kabul's laboratory equipment for performing water quality and water level measurements does not work reliably, so monitoring is not performed regularly. The situation is similar or worse in Herat, Kandahar and Mazar-e-Sharif, where information is sparse or non-existent. Local authorities generally do not have the resources and qualified staff necessary to conduct groundwater monitoring. On the positive side, information about groundwater is becoming more readily available as a result of studies being conducted by the World Bank and other international organizations currently working in Afghanistan. WHO is also working with the Ministry of Public Health to improve water testing and monitoring capacity. Nevertheless, until Afghanistan develops comprehensive groundwater monitoring programmes, its water supplies will continue to be degraded and depleted.

Drinking water quality: Water samples taken by UNEP detected high concentrations of two bacteriological contaminants: total coliforms and *E. coli*. The general conclusion is that Afghanistan's urban drinking water supplies appear to be severely compromised. As noted earlier, samples from Kabul's water distribution network and wells found *E. coli* and coliform values ranging from 18 to over 100 counts in 100 ml of water. Two samples drawn from private wells (one 14 m deep, the other 25 m deep) were also contaminated with *E. coli* and total coliforms. Four other samples came from a United Nations building: all – including one from newly filtered water – were contaminated with total coliforms and one (unfiltered) with *E. coli*. These findings are in line with UNICEF tests which found that fecal bacteria infected 70 per cent of Kabul's shallow wells. A similar picture emerged in Mazar-e-Sharif where *E. coli* contamination was found in samples taken at a mosque, from a municipal groundwater supply, at a water treatment plant, and from taps. These samples also contained nitrate levels at or above the WHO guideline of 50 mg/l. In Herat, UNEP samples again found tap water containing high levels of total coliform and nitrate levels twice the WHO standard. One sample from a deep well contained 5 counts of *E. coli* in 100 ml of water. More encouraging results were found in Kandahar: although one well sample found 4 counts of total coliforms in 100 ml of water, three other samples did not detect contamination.

Water quality monitoring: Little is known about the quality of the country's urban water supplies because monitoring is not carried out on a regular formal basis. For a number of reasons, drinking water analyses are almost impossible to perform, due mainly to a lack of laboratory infrastructure and the fact that urban water authorities are generally lacking in qualified expertise and resources. As a result, consistent and reliable water-quality data are very difficult to obtain. In Mazar-e-Sharif, for example, the local water authority analyses drinking water from the public network (which supplies half the city) every second month. And while Herat's mobile laboratory monitors total coliforms, pH and turbidity of water from nine locations weekly, it lacks the resources to monitor other important parametres, such as *E. coli*, typhus and cholera. The NGO Agroaction has developed a laboratory for water quality testing, and is working to increase the level of knowledge on water quality.

Water quality management: Poor water quality management, allowing polluted wastewater to routinely infiltrate drinking water distribution systems, is damaging Afghanistan's precious drinking water resources. Furthermore, at a management level, no connection is being

Drinking water samples analysed in Mazar-e-Sharif using portable equipment

DENNIS BRUHN/UNEP, 2002

AFGHANISTAN

made between waste management and drinking water management. Fundamental measures, such as establishing sanitary protection zones around drinking water sources, are not being taken. Kabul, for example, is supplied by four major well fields, but none of them have sanitary protection zones near the water intakes – and one is located just 1 km from the city's waste dumpsite. A similar situation exists in Herat where the city's treated supply reaches 30 per cent of the city from eight deep wells, none of which have sanitary protection zones. In Mazar-e-Sharif, UNEP visited a well field located 20 m from a sewage canal and 200 m from a destroyed oil storage facility. Kandahar has a particularly strong need to manage its resources carefully since it depends exclusively on unchlorinated groundwater supplies.

Analysis of drinking water samples in Mazar-e-Sharif using portable equipment

Water supply: Afghanistan's urban water supply networks are highly inefficient. Kabul's supply was severely damaged during the many years of conflict and regular maintenance has been absent. It loses as much as 60 per cent of its supply due to leaks and illegal use. It covers perhaps a quarter of the city's population and operates for only eight hours a day due to electricity shortages. Kandahar's network, which serves 30 per cent of the city six hours per day, loses an estimated 70 per cent of the water through leaks. Because the water service is not metered, there are no incentives for water conservation, causing water to be wasted when it is available. In Herat, drinking water is supplied by one public network. It loses 30 per cent of its supply to leaks in the system and only 10 per cent of its 150 public taps are functional. Mazar-e-Sharif's system is also in very bad condition: the main network serves less than half of the city's residents for only four hours per day due to power shortages. The rest of the population relies principally on shallow wells that tend to be heavily laden with biological and chemical contaminants. Each well serves an average of 120 families, and more than half the wells' hand pumps do not function reliably.

Drought effects: During the last four years of drought there has been almost no precipitation to recharge the groundwater aquifers, and so the groundwater table has dropped significantly throughout Afghanistan. A local analysis reviewed by UNEP indicates that the groundwater level in Kabul, for example, has fallen by 1.7-4.6 m in the last three years. In Kandahar, the water table is dropping at an estimated 1-8 m per year and several shallow wells have dried out. The range of values in both cases depend on local geological and hydrological conditions. A large number of new and deeper wells are currently being established, but local authorities (and the international community) have no systematic plans for the managed extraction of groundwater resources. When UNEP visited Kandahar's northern residential areas, it was difficult to find a well that was not dry, despite the fact that most of the shallow wells were created in 1998.

Post-Conflict Environmental Assessment

International assistance: Improving access to drinking water has clearly been a focal point of the international community during recent years. However, almost all of the international community's efforts have been implemented without proper policy guidance or coordination. As already described, in some cases drinking water wells have been dug next to septic tanks, or without considering impacts on nearby shallow wells. Nevertheless, a number of important positive steps have been taken. For example, the International Committee of the Red Cross (ICRC) is providing Herat with various forms of assistance that will rehabilitate the city's water supply system. UNICEF has helped Herat to chlorinate its water, and according to the local water authority this has resulted in a significant decrease in cholera. The German development bank Kreditanstalt für Wiederaufbau (KfW) is currently working in Kabul to provide new pumps, repair electric generators, and reconstruct pipelines and water reservoirs. The project's goal is to restore the city's supply to pre-conflict levels, which would cover 60 per cent of the city's current population. In addition, the World Bank has completed a study of basic infrastructure needs in 12 cities, including Kandahar, Herat and Mazar-e-Sharif, and emergency assistance is anticipated.

■ Public facilities and industrial sites

UNEP investigated a number of hospitals, factories and other industrial sites in each of the cities visited, looking for pollution 'hotspots' that threaten human health. Several of the sites posed no threat to public health and the environment, while others presented disturbing pictures of environmental negligence that may be severely damaging to human health and the environment.

Key findings:

Hospitals

HERAT REGIONAL HOSPITAL

Herat Regional Hospital is located in the centre of Herat. In general, the overall standard of the 400-bed facility is reasonable, but the hospital is plagued by extremely high-risk waste management practices.

Clinical waste is carried around the hospital in open plastic buckets by staff lacking protective clothing. This practice alone could easily lead to the airborne spread of infection and disease to the hospital's staff, patients and many daily visitors. Outside, the contents of the buckets are either emptied into wheelbarrows or carried directly across the hospital grounds to an incinerator. Not surprisingly, the hospital grounds are littered with clinical debris. Much of this activity occurs within feet of visitors and patients.

The waste deposition point adjacent to the incinerator is open, easily accessed and awash with medical waste, including syringes and other hazardous items. Insects crawl over rotting, blood-soaked swabs. During UNEP's visit to the site, a small girl was playing on top of the waste piled in the deposition area. Perhaps worst of all, there appears to be a complete lack of awareness of the environmental and public health risks posed by these waste management practices.

In addition, the hospital's incinerator is very basic, and apparently unable to cope with the volume of waste generated by the hospital. Although hospital staff told UNEP that the incinerator is not currently in use, fuel is currently stacked nearby. The inadequacy of the incinerator in terms of burning temperatures and conditions mean that emissions might well contain viruses, bacteria, toxic chemicals, heavy metals and dioxins that are blown over the hospital grounds when in use. Waste not incinerated is collected by the municipality and dumped in the city's landfill.

The hospital's water supply is in very poor condition. Drinking water for patients and visitors is taken from several hand-pump wells that draw on a shallow aquifer. Water for other uses in the hospital comes from a deep aquifer. Water samples taken by UNEP from the hospital's operating room, a deep-water well and one of the hospital's hand-pump wells found contamination from *E. coli*, total coliforms and high concentrations of nitrate. Contamination of water used in the operating room obviously poses an extraordinary hazard to patients undergoing surgery, as well as to hospital staff.

The hospital's water distribution network has leaks in several pipeline valves and connection pits. Most of the pits with leaks were unsealed, and various types of waste had been thrown into them. In addition, the water supply is only pressurized for eight hours per day, which contributes to the potential for wastewater infiltration.

The hospital has two large underground oil storage tanks. One is located only 10 m from the hospital's deep-water well, posing a clear threat of cross-contamination. A soil sample taken by UNEP at this location found 135 000 mg/kg of total hydrocarbons – significant contamination due probably to either a leak in the tank or pipeline, or spills during the filling process. A sample taken from the nearby deep-water well, however, found no contamination by hydrocarbons, indicating that contamination had not yet reached the groundwater table. However, this is likely to occur at some stage, depending on future rainfall conditions and groundwater recharge.

An electricity generating station is also located less than 15 m from the deep-water well. Fuel has leaked in different parts of the station, including inside a manifold room that is closest to the well. The danger of cross-contamination is evident.

A small oil-drum storage area is located in the same vicinity. A soil sample taken by UNEP near this site found 826 000 mg/kg of total hydrocarbons. Such localized contamination is

SOREN HVILSHØJ/UNEP, 2002

Collection point for medical waste at Herat Region Hospital

Post-Conflict Environmental Assessment

► Cross-contamination of groundwater resources at Herat hospital

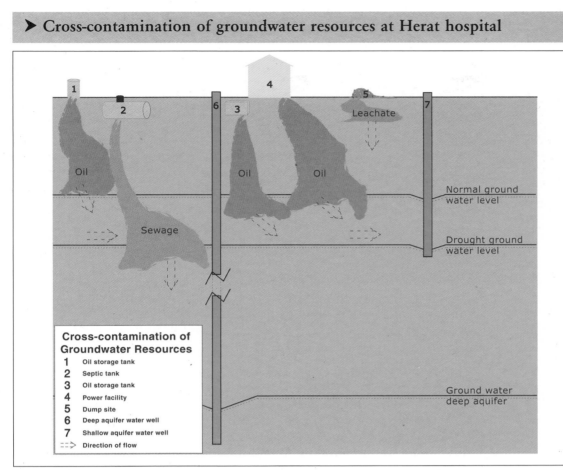

Cross-contamination of groundwater resources is an extremely serious problem throughout Afghanistan. The situation at Herat Regional Hospital is representative of many urban locations. When groundwaters return to normal levels, the amount of water contamination is likely to increase.

to be expected given the potential for spillage during the filling process, both of the subterranean tank and from the decanting of oil drums.

The hospital's wastewater is collected in a large septic tank. The integrity of this tank is not known, however its proximity to groundwater resources poses an obvious danger of infiltration and contamination.

MAZAR-E-SHARIF CIVIL HOSPITAL

The 300-bed Mazar-e-Sharif Civil Hospital, which receives 2 000 patients daily, is situated in a badly deteriorating building and has equipment of the lowest quality. Its environmental management practices are extremely poor.

Debris from the rooms is washed along the corridors and out into a drain, which leads to a huge underground septic tank. There are three similar tanks in the hospital grounds, all full of solid and liquid waste. The municipality empties the septic tank on request, but this service is unreliable, raising grave concerns about soil and groundwater degradation and human exposure to medical waste contamination.

The municipality collects the hospital's non-medical waste, but these loads frequently include medical waste as well. Due to a lack of storage or incineration facilities, organs or limbs that are removed from patients are frequently returned after the operation. The health risks of this practice are uncertain.

AFGHANISTAN

Well in Mazar-e-Sharif Civil Hospital filled with medical wastes.

SCOTT CROSSETT/UNEP, 2002

The hospital's main water supply comes from a deep well located in the hospital grounds. Water samples taken by UNEP from the hospital's operating room found high levels of total coliform and *E. coli* and equally high nitrate contamination – an extremely disturbing finding from a public health standpoint.

After water from a 15-m well in the hospital grounds turned poor in quality, the hospital began filling the well with medical waste. Such activity poses a serious risk of contamination of the groundwater aquifer. A new hand-pump well was drilled about 50 m away, which the hospital is now using to supply drinking water to the public. A water sample taken by UNEP from the new well also found contamination from nitrate, fecal coliform and *E. coli*.

MIRWAIS CIVILIAN HOSPITAL

The 300-bed Mirwais Civilian Hospital in Kandahar is the only general hospital in the province and, as such, cares for patients from the city and rural areas.

The hospital separates surgical waste, which is disposed of through a private contract with ICRC. All other waste is dumped in a site within the hospital grounds and, with the exception of needles, is burned in a small incinerator operated by the Ministry of Public Health. Needles are deposited in a concrete vault in the ground adjacent to the incinerator. Plastic waste is used to start the fire and bring the temperature in the incinerator up to the required degree, producing dangerous dioxin and furan air emissions in the process. Since the incinerator only works during the day, the pile of waste, which is added to throughout the day and into the night, will continue to grow in size.

The hospital's water supply comes from two sources: a deep groundwater well

SCOTT CROSSETT/UNEP, 2002

Incinerator at Mirwais Civilian Hospital, Kandahar

3

and the main municipal supply. The two supplies are fed into a single tank on the hospital premises. While the quality of the groundwater supply is very good, a drinking water sample taken by UNEP from the hospital's laboratory found 50 mg/l of nitrate – just at the WHO threshold of acceptability.

The hospital's wastewater is fed into an open, tree and shrub-filled pond from which it soaks into the ground. A system of 40 tanks collects the resulting effluent/sediment mix. This sludge is regularly removed and fed into a soak-away system. After the sludge has dried, it is disposed of on land. The application of medical waste sludge to land is a high-risk activity that could contaminate groundwater sources and create public health risks.

Oil facilities

SHIBURGHAN OIL REFINERIES

The Shiburghan Oil Refineries are a conglomerate of small-scale private oil refineries located about 100 km west of Mazar-e-Sharif. The refineries comprise 118 individual units, each with 4–5 boilers using gas heating. The units produce 50–60 barrels of refined oil per week. The operations are managed with no regard for environmental impact or worker safety. As a result, the air, soil and groundwater around the site is highly contaminated with a variety of oil products.

Pipelines extend from the boilers to a long water basin in which refined oil products are condensed. The outcome of the process is petroleum, gasoline and diesel, and a coal-like sludge residue from the crude-oil cracking (heating and separation) process. The sludge is apparently sold for domestic heating and as fuel for local brick factories. When burned, the sludge produces a thick black smoke similar to that produced by burning rubber. A sample of the residue taken by UNEP found approximately 10 mg/kg of sulphur. When used in domestic heating, the burned residue emits sulphur dioxide (SO_2) and hydrocarbon compounds that can cause respiratory illnesses. Given the large extent to which the by-product is used in urban areas such as Mazar-e-Sharif, the risk to public health must be high.

Pollution of the soil is very high around the refineries. Crude oil spilt near all the boilers, and spillage of refined oil products generally and particularly in areas where barrels are stored are the prime causes. Stored waste products are also contaminating the soil. A soil sample taken at the site found 83 000 mg/kg of

Boilers leaking crude oil onto the ground at Shiburghan

SØREN HVILSHØJ/UNEP, 2002

AFGHANISTAN

41

hydrocarbons, highlighting the obvious and significant pollution risk to the area's groundwater supplies.

MAWLAWY OIL STORAGE FACILITY

The Mawlawy oil storage facility, situated on mountain slopes north of Herat, is polluting local water supplies and threatening the health of nearby residents.

Oil is stored at two sites. The first is used for unloading, storing and reloading of crude oil, diesel and benzene. It has 58 active small tanks and 6 inactive large tanks, all located on the surface. The tanks have a combined storage capacity of about 4 million litres. Every day approximately ten trucks, primarily from Iran and Turkmenistan, deliver 20 m^3 of oil product to the facility. There is evident spillage around the unloading station and leakage from several of the oil storage tanks. A soil sample taken by UNEP found 46 000 mg/kg of hydrocarbons, indicating severe oil pollution.

DENNIS BRUHN/UNEP, 2002

Mawlawy oil storage facility for benzene and petroleum, Herat

The second oil storage area is an underground facility used for benzene and petroleum. It comprises 20 tanks, each 50–75 m^3 in size, providing a total storage capacity of 1 million litres. Leakage from the underground tanks was determined visually, but it was not possible to assess the extent of this pollution due to lack of access.

Judging from the topography of the site, the groundwater would appear to flow from the oil storage facility towards the city of Herat. A water sample taken by UNEP from a residential well downstream of the storage site found a hydrocarbon concentration of 0.05 mg/l. To place this in context, this measure is above the maximum Danish and German standards for drinking water by a factor of five. The well-water also contained levels of *E. coli* and coliform contamination above 100 counts of bacteria in 100 ml of water.

SAR-E-POL CRUDE OIL TERMINAL

The Sar-e-Pol crude oil terminal, located in the Mazar-e-Sharif region, receives approximately 70 tonnes of crude oil per day via pipelines from Shiburghan and nearby oil fields. Approximately four truckloads per day are filled at the terminal. There is also an onsite refinery which has not been used in more than a decade.

The terminal – in particular the oil storage tanks and filling station – is a source of severe soil pollution. Because there were no wells in the area, the condition of the groundwater could not be determined precisely. Spilled crude oil floats to a collection pond, from which it either evaporates into the atmosphere or seeps into the ground. There is a clear risk of contamination of shallow groundwater aquifers; a risk that will increase in the event of precipitation.

Post-Conflict Environmental Assessment

Oil spilt on ground at Sar-e-Pol oil terminal, Mazar-e-Sharif

SØREN HVILSHOJ/UNEP, 2002

The area downstream of the terminal is used principally for agriculture, where surface water supplies are used for irrigation. UNEP was unable to locate drinking water wells in the immediate downstream area. There was no visual sign of oil in either the irrigation canals or the river. A water sample taken from a point in the river approximately 500 m downstream found no significant hydrocarbon contamination, but did find levels of *E. coli* and total coliform contamination above 100 counts of bacteria in 100 ml of water.

Other industrial facilities

ZHORA PLASTIC RECYCLING/SHOE FACTORY

The Zhora Plastic Recycling/ Shoe Factory operates from the basement of a small block of multi-storey flats in a residential district near the centre of Kabul. The facility is one of ten similar structures in the immediate area. Noxious fumes from the process undoubtedly permeate the residential quarters nearby. In addition, chemical waste from the facility is dumped into a hole in the ground adjacent to the factory site, a practice that is sure to be severely degrading groundwater sources.

The factory operation relies exclusively on child labour to produce 600 shoes per day. It employs 20 children in two shifts that maintains output 24 hours per day. The children spend

SCOTT CROSSETT/UNEP, 2002

Children recycling plastics

URBAN ENVIRONMENT

AFGHANISTAN

43

their days grinding discarded plastic shoes into a granulated mix, after which they add a chemical softener that liquefies the plastic. The liquid plastic is then poured into a mould which forms the new shoes. Finally, the shoes are coated with a cellulose-based black dye that produces a shiny black finish. The children work without protection, enduring constant overexposure to the process chemicals. At the end of their shift period, they sleep at their machines or in alcoves within the factory – a rest from the hardship of work but not from its toxic environment.

Child sleeping in a Kabul shoe factory

The site's appalling environmental and labour conditions are indicative of the magnitude of Afghanistan's development challenges.

SHIBURGAN BRICK FACTORY

Afghanistan's brick factories, of which there are many in and around cities, pump a great deal of air pollution into an urban atmosphere already heavily polluted by traffic-related emissions.

During UNEP's visit to the brick factory in Shiburghan, the factory was in full production, releasing thick black smoke that could be seen for miles around. The air smelled of paraf-

Black smoke from brick factory in Shiburghan

Post-Conflict Environmental Assessment

fin. Factory management said that they were burning a grass-type product for fuel. Although the brick factories are obviously important sources of employment, they are contributing significant amounts of air pollution, posing risks of respiratory illness for workers and local residents.

ZURI BATTERY COMPANY

The Zuri Battery Company is a family-operated business located outside Herat. Occupying a series of new and well-kept buildings, the factory manufactures approximately 400 automobile batteries every day.

In general, the manufacturing process is well run, the facility is clean and some steps have been taken toward environmental management, including recycling and materials recovery. There are, however, several serious environmental conditions that require immediate attention. For example, gas fumes make breathing difficult in an unvented area where approximately 100 batteries are charged daily. The factory is recovering lead from spent batteries and storing plastic and oxide in anticipation of future recycling capabilities. A sample of dust taken from the floor of the battery recycling room found a high lead content of 300–400 mg/kg, as well as arsenic, copper, zinc and antimony. A small lead smelter in the recycling area melts the lead before it is poured into moulds for cooling. The smelter smokestack does not have scrubbers, allowing lead-contaminated emissions to escape into the atmosphere.

Lead dust threatens the health of workers at Zuri battery factory in Herat

All of these aspects pose obvious health risks to the environment and to the factory's five core workers, all of whom appeared not to be wearing the protective clothing that had been provided by the company.

HERAT ASPHALT FACTORY

A state-owned asphalt factory located approximately 10 km from Herat is a source of intense air pollution. The factory employs 100 people and is now producing 40 tonnes of road asphalt per hour, more than double the amount produced under the Taliban regime. The company also employs two road repair teams, each with about 70 employees.

The Herat factory consumes approximately 1 000 litres of crude oil and 3 000 litres of diesel daily. UNEP observed poor maintenance of the pipelines and heavy oil leaks from barrels onto unprotected ground. Water is supplied by truck and stored in an onsite water reservoir. Asphalt for road construction usually mixes a heated asphalt binder with stones, gravel and lime. A sample taken by UNEP indicated that the dust and asphalt binders being used at the plant were of bitumen. The chemical substances in bitumen, including poly aromatic hydrocarbons (PAHs) are known to have hazardous impacts on human health including cancer. However, the factory's management reported that their manufacturing processes produce no waste products.

AFGHANISTAN

Oil tanks at asphalt factory in Herat leaking heavy oil onto unprotected ground

SØREN HVILSHØJ/UNEP, 2002

On the day UNEP visited the plant, dense smoke was pouring into the atmosphere, coming primarily from the heaters of the asphalt binder. Smoke was also being emitted from the mixing unit. The chimney smoke and general smell of oil products in the area made it clear that the plant was contributing a heavy load of pollution to the atmosphere. The wind was blowing the emissions in the direction of neighbouring settlements.

SØREN HVILSHØJ/UNEP, 2002

Heavy black smoke rises from the asphalt factory in Herat

Management is aware that the asphalt factory does not use best available technology. They are aware also that asphalt plants in other countries, such as Iran, produce significantly less air pollution. Management also acknowledged that the plant's poor working conditions have caused health problems, and they expressed strong interest in creating a health centre for employees.

Judging from the topography of the site, it is unlikely that the groundwater is flowing towards immediate human settlements. However, the plant is located in a valley and the direction of water flow is towards the city of Herat. No information was available about the groundwater table.

At the time, there was no surface water in the riverbed, due to drought. It is possible that the plant's severe soil pollution (at least of the topsoil) could lead to surface water degradation in the event of precipitation.

■ Air quality

Dust and vehicle emissions in Afghanistan's urban areas are the main factors negatively affecting air quality. Current assessments of vehicle density in the country amount to 500 000 cars, 30 000 buses and 50 000 trucks – figures that are growing rapidly. Most run on low-grade diesel and cause problems of air pollution that are very evident in urban centres.

During late autumn and winter, air quality is reportedly worsened by domestic emissions arising from increased use of ovens, stoves and open fires. Electricity shortages and a lack of fuelwood mean that households resort to burning some packaging materials that may cause toxic fumes.

Key findings:

UNEP carried out air sampling at a number of urban sites in Kandahar, Mazar-e-Sharif, Kabul and Herat. The results indicate high amounts of dust and concentrations of poly aromatic hydrocarbons (PAHs) at all sites. At the time of sampling, PAH air pollution was most likely originating from vehicle exhaust emissions from nearly 600 000 vehicles nationwide. Benzo-a-pyrene is one of the pollutants detected and is believed to increase risk of lung cancer. The highest concentrations were detected in Mazar-e-Sharif, where analyses show 13.6 Ng/m^3. The WHO average values for urban areas range from 1 to 10 Ng/m^3. Concentrations for Kabul and Kandahar were between these values, while those for Herat were below WHO average values.

The potential risks to human health from PAHs through inhalation are increased by the presence of dust in the air. Dust binds hydrocarbon particles, prevents them escaping into the upper atmosphere, and increases the likelihood of human exposure. Many residents reported that the amount of dust in all the major cities has increased in the last four years. On extremely dusty days, people resort to masks or cloth for protection from the dust. A combination of drought and loss of vegetation are contributing factors to the increased dust levels.

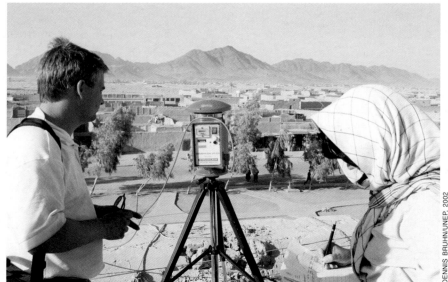

Air sampling along Kandahar's main street

DENNIS BRUHN/UNEP, 2002

AFGHANISTAN

4

Natural resources

Introduction

In a country where over 80 per cent of the population relies directly on the natural resource base to meet their daily needs, widespread environmental degradation poses an immense threat to future livelihoods. During over two decades of conflict, Afghanistan's natural resource base has been heavily damaged by military activities, refugee movements, over-exploitation, and a lack of management and institutional capacity. The past three to four years of drought have worsened this damage.

Restoring the country's environment is vital for the long-term well-being of the Afghan people. The principal goal of land and biodiversity management must be to improve food security and contribute to poverty alleviation, while at the same time protecting the integrity of ecosystems. In many cases, long-term ecological damage has been caused, for example to groundwater or soil resources, as people rush to meet immediate humanitarian needs such as water and food. While this approach has alleviated short-term suffering, in many cases it will further exacerbate the humanitarian situation in the long term, as degraded groundwater aquifers and eroded soils may take centuries to recover.

With the development of the new administration in Afghanistan, a vital opportunity exists to assess the state of the land and its resources. The new administration urgently needs an information base on which to plan a new era of resource management, making wise use of the country's land, water and biological resources to improve the lives of its people and protect its ecological systems.

With these needs in mind, UNEP's objective was to conduct a rapid assessment of water and wetlands, forests and woodlands, protected areas, and wildlife. The results would help to increase knowledge of the status of Afghanistan's natural resource base, identify the key pressures and threats to sustainable use, and enable UNEP to recommend priority actions for follow-up by the Afghan government and its partners.

Between 6 September and 10 October 2002 UNEP's international experts and Afghan advisers visited the following key sites in each thematic area:

- **Wetlands**: the Helmand River and western Amu Darya basins, including the Sistan wetlands;

- **Forests**: northern pistachio and juniper woodlands in the provinces of Herat, Badghis, Kunduz

Deforestation and overgrazing have contributed to serious soil erosion at this site near Qala-i-Nau

and Takhar, and one *tugai* forested island in the Amu Darya River near Imam Sahib. Conifer forests in the eastern provinces of Nuristan, Kunar and Nangarhar were assessed using satellite imagery as ongoing conflict prevented access;

- **Protected areas**: Band-e-Amir National Park, Kole Hashmat Khan, and Dasht-e-Nawar and Ab-e-Estada Waterfowl and Flamingo Sanctuaries; and

- **Wakhan Corridor:** including Pamir-e-Buzurg wildlife reserve.

UNEP's field investigations employed a variety of techniques. These included desk studies of existing information, including the results of the joint UNDP/FAO studies in the late 1970s[26][27][28][29][30][31][32][33][34] and a preliminary assessment of environmental conditions in 2000 made by Save the Environment Afghanistan (SEA)[35]. Recent environmental studies by Afghan scientists[36] were also included. Maps, satellite imagery, geographic information systems (GIS), field observations including soil, water and dust samples, and repeat photography using images from 1977[37][38] also provided valuable information. Other data were gathered by interviewing government officials, local people, and relevant non-governmental organizations and UN agencies.

Principal findings and conclusions

■ Water and wetlands

With rainfall low and erratic in much of Afghanistan, and large areas qualifying as desert or semi-desert, rivers, streams and other wetlands are crucial for human needs such as drinking water and agriculture, and for maintaining populations of wild plants and animals, many of which provide potential for economic opportunities.

Pumping groundwater in Kandahar

Although broad calculations suggest that, in average conditions, Afghanistan as a whole uses less than one-third of its potential 75 000 million m³ water resources[39], regional differences in supply, inefficient use, and wastage mean that a major part of the country experiences water scarcity. The recent years of conflict have made it difficult or impossible to make improvements to infrastructure or to integrate uncoordinated local schemes into a coherent national strategy for water. However, improved water resource management will, in many regions, be an essential first step in rebuilding rural communities.

UNEP focused its field assessment efforts on understanding current pressures on water resources in two of the largest and most significant water catchments: the Helmand basin in the southwest and Amu Darya in the north. Four wetland zones previously given protected area status were also visited: Band-e-Amir, Kole Hashmat Khan, Dasht-e-Nawar and Ab-e-Estada.

Helmand River basin

The Helmand River rises in the southern Hindu Kush and, flowing south and west, drains about 31 per cent of the country's land area. The river crosses the extensive dry lands in southwest Afghanistan, looping below the Dasht-e-Margo desert to enter the Sistan basin. Wetlands in this massive natural depression, stretching north–south for some 200 km, have supported irrigated agriculture since at least 3 000 BC. Approximately 13 per cent of the country's irrigated areas lie in the Helmand basin, where intensive industrial crop production and commercial horticulture is commonly practised[40].

The Helmand River typically rises between March and June, rapidly recharging first the easternmost lake, Hamoun-i-Puzak (its southern third lying within Iran), followed by Hamoun-e-Sabari to the west (half in Iran) and Hamoun-e-Helmand (entirely in Iran). An enormous saltpan, the Gaud-e-Zireh, lies below the Helmand's southern section. From time to time it receives water from the Hamoun-e-Helmand via the Shela (said to be a former channel of the Helmand) and by direct overspill from the Helmand.

The wetland area varies significantly from year to year, depending on the volume of water supplied by the Helmand, Khash Rud and Farah Rud Rivers, as well as the other feeder streams to the north. In years of exceptionally high water, the wetlands can cover up to 4 000 square kilometres[41], reaching their greatest extent with spring floods. However, the lakes have also disappeared completely in the past. For example, the Boundary Commission found the lakes and the lower Helmand dry in 1902 and witnessed their refilling in 1903[42].

Despite evident recession in the area regularly cropped, the Sistan region has remained an important source of agricultural production (chiefly cropland and cattle, which graze in the reed marshes) and a source of fish and waterbirds for food. It is also an internationally important haven for wetland wildlife – the Iranian side was designated as a Ramsar site in 1975[43]. Up to half-a-million waterfowl were counted on Hamoun-i-Puzak in the 1970s[44], representing roughly 150 species of migrating and non-migrating birds[45]. Eight globally threatened waterfowl species formerly spent the winter on the lakes, among them Dalmatian pelican (*Pelecanus crispus*) and marbled teal (*Marmaronetta angustirostris*). The diversity of bird life in the wetlands was almost matched by nearly 140 species of fish that supported bird, mammal and human populations[46].

View of Helmand River near Lashkar Gah

Post-Conflict Environmental Assessment

In medieval times, Zaranj was a major cultural centre but it now stands isolated while ruins dot the surrounding desert. Its prosperity was based on a network of feeder canals that distributed water conserved behind a low dam across the Helmand south of the city. Although the system was damaged after the invasion of King Timur in the 14th century, it appears that the combined effects of sedimentation, salinization and changes in the course of the Helmand were already reducing productivity[47]. The notorious 'wind of 120 days', which blows from the northwest between May and September, scours the landscape, driving banks of mobile sand and adding to instability in the drainage network.

Within the past five years, the Helmand River has experienced dramatic declines in water flows. In 2001, the river ran at 98 per cent below its annual average[48]. With declining precipitation, the snowfields that supply the headwaters of the Helmand shrank from 41 000 km^2 to 26 000 km^2 between 1998 and 2000[49]. With continued withdrawals for irrigated agriculture, Helmand waters failed to reach the Sistan basin altogether in 2001. This led to complete desiccation of the wetlands and has had a severe impact on the Sistan environment.

> **Water flow of the Helmand River, 1991–2001[48]**

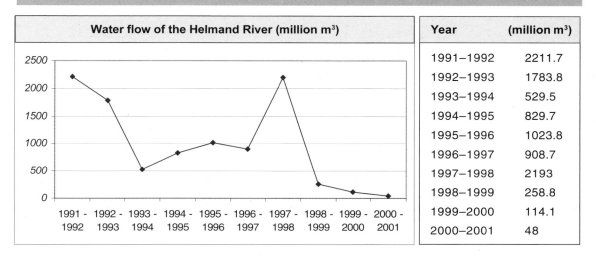

Water flow of the Helmand River (million m³)

Year	(million m³)
1991–1992	2211.7
1992–1993	1783.8
1993–1994	529.5
1994–1995	829.7
1995–1996	1023.8
1996–1997	908.7
1997–1998	2193
1998–1999	258.8
1999–2000	114.1
2000–2001	48

UNEP visited key sites within the Helmand basin and Sistan wetlands to assess the prevailing environmental conditions. Satellite image analyses was conducted to determine the extent of degradation to the Sistan wetlands and potential for recovery. The status of transboundary agreements was also investigated.

Key findings:

Desiccation of Sistan wetlands: Local residents reported to UNEP that lake Hamoun-i-Puzak has been dry for the previous four years due to the drought and poor water management upstream. Furthermore, it was reported that prior to the drought the flow in all of the rivers feeding the wetlands has been drastically reduced, by up to 70 per cent in some cases[50]. UNEP observed a variety of reedbeds to be completely dry, and residents reported that waterfowl have largely deserted the area. Wolves, jackals, hedgehogs and wild boar *(Sus scrofa)* were reported to be numerous, while wildcats and porcupine were said to be rare. UNEP obtained Landsat satellite images for the years 1976, 1987, 1998 and 2001 to verify the current condition of the wetlands and to compare it with previous years. Image analyses revealed that 99 per cent of the wetland has dried since 1998, including Hamoun-i-Puzak, Hamoun-e-Sabari and Hamoun-e-Helmand. Each of the main rivers feeding the wetland, including the Helmand, Farah Rud and Khash Rud, also appeared to be completely dry. However, the analyses also demonstrated that the wetlands have undergone significant desiccation in the past, and have recovered with the return of the rains. In 1987, for example,

Dried reedbeds of the Sistan wetlands

RENE NIJENHUIS/UNEP, 2002

73 per cent of the wetland area was completely dry. Yet by 1998 the wetlands and surrounding vegetation had almost completely recovered, once again providing important wildlife habitat and agricultural inputs. This finding suggests that the wetlands may have the potential to make a recovery, when rainfall returns to the region. However, improving water management in the entire basin will be a prerequisite for success.

Erosion and sedimentation: Without a stable source of water over the past four years, much of the natural vegetation of the basin has died or been collected for fuel. This has contributed to soil erosion and significant movement of sand onto roads and into settlements, and irrigated areas. Up to 100 villages have been submerged by wind-blown dust and sand[51]. Many agricultural fields have also been affected. UNEP investigated sand movement along the border of the Registan desert in 1986 and 2002. The results indicate significant sand movement in a westward direction and loss of agricultural areas. Dust and sediments are also reported to be filling-in irrigation canals and lakebeds, as well as the reservoirs at Dahla and Kajaki dams. To determine the extent of the sedimentation in Hamoun-i-Puzak, UNEP compared the current location of reedbeds with descriptions from 1888[52]. The results appear to indicate that the Helmand delta has advanced up to 20 km north as a result of sedimentation. If the sedimentation continues, the risks are clear: as the storage capacity of the lakes, reservoirs and irrigation networks is reduced, opportunities to store water will be lost and, at the same time, vulnerability to both drought and flooding will increase.

RENE NIJENHUIS/UNEP, 2002

Boat buried in sand in former water channel near Kang

> **Satellite image analysis of Sistan basin wetland change**

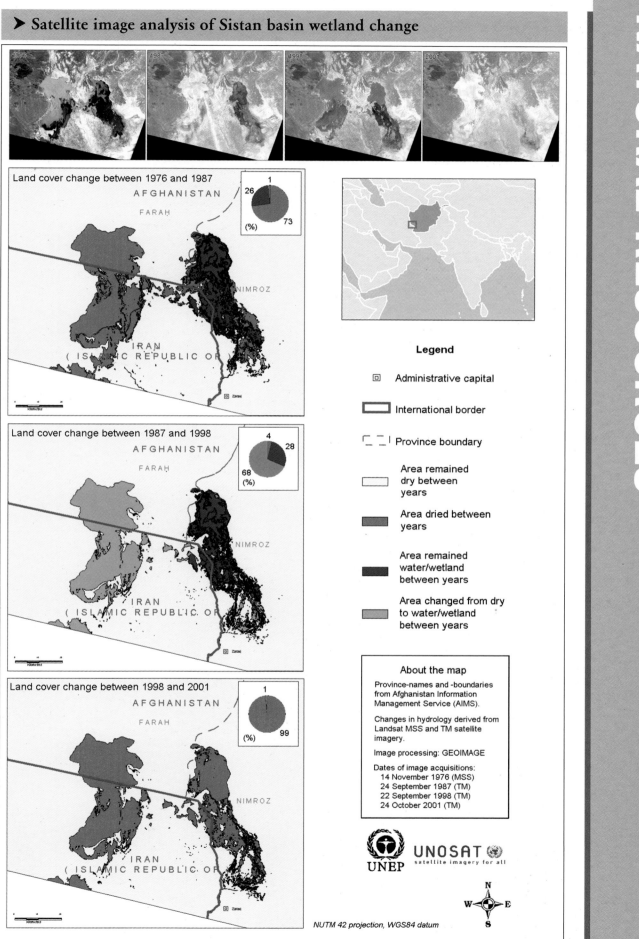

Land cover change between 1976 and 1987

AFGHANISTAN
FARAH
NIMROZ
IRAN
(ISLAMIC REPUBLIC OF)
Zaranj

1
26
73
(%)

Land cover change between 1987 and 1998

AFGHANISTAN
FARAH
NIMROZ
IRAN
(ISLAMIC REPUBLIC OF)
Zaranj

4
28
68
(%)

Land cover change between 1998 and 2001

AFGHANISTAN
FARAH
NIMROZ
IRAN
(ISLAMIC REPUBLIC OF)
Zaranj

1
99
(%)

Legend

◙ Administrative capital

▭ International border

⌐ ¬ Province boundary

☐ Area remained dry between years

■ Area dried between years

■ Area remained water/wetland between years

■ Area changed from dry to water/wetland between years

About the map

Province-names and -boundaries from Afghanistan Information Management Service (AIMS).

Changes in hydrology derived from Landsat MSS and TM satellite imagery.

Image processing: GEOIMAGE

Dates of image acquisitions:
  14 November 1976 (MSS)
  24 September 1987 (TM)
  22 September 1998 (TM)
  24 October 2001 (TM)

UNEP   UNOSAT
satellite imagery for all

NUTM 42 projection, WGS84 datum

N
W E
S

AFGHANISTAN

4

➤ Satellite imagery of the Sistan basin, 1976

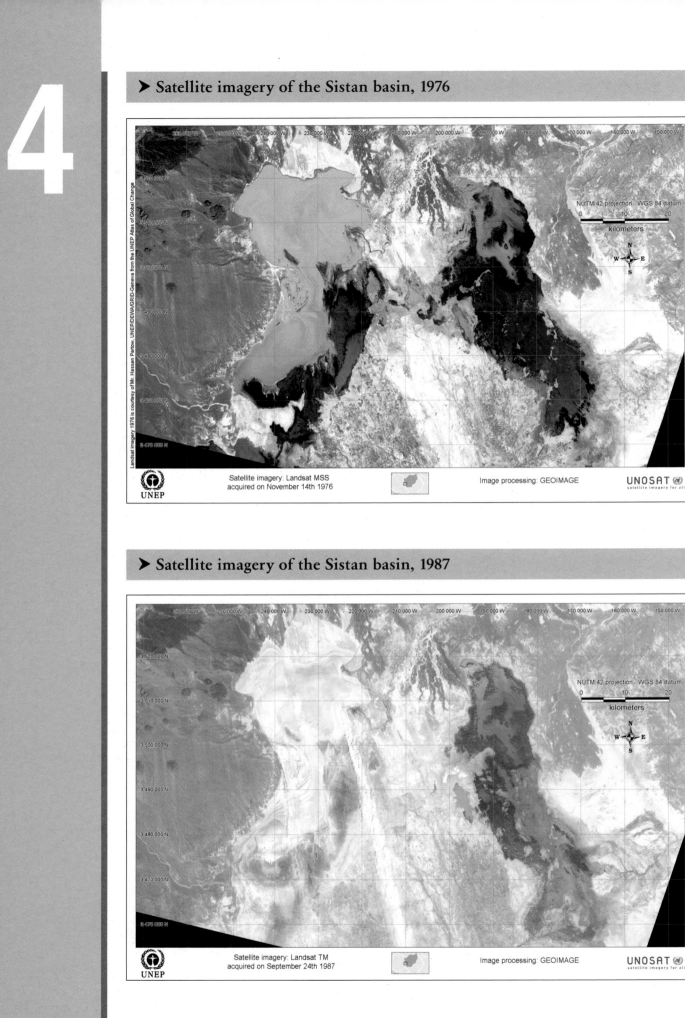

Satellite imagery: Landsat MSS
acquired on November 14th 1976

Image processing: GEOIMAGE

UNEP

UNOSAT
satellite imagery for all

➤ Satellite imagery of the Sistan basin, 1987

Satellite imagery: Landsat TM
acquired on September 24th 1987

Image processing: GEOIMAGE

UNEP

UNOSAT
satellite imagery for all

Post-Conflict Environmental Assessment

➤ Satellite imagery of the Sistan basin, 1998

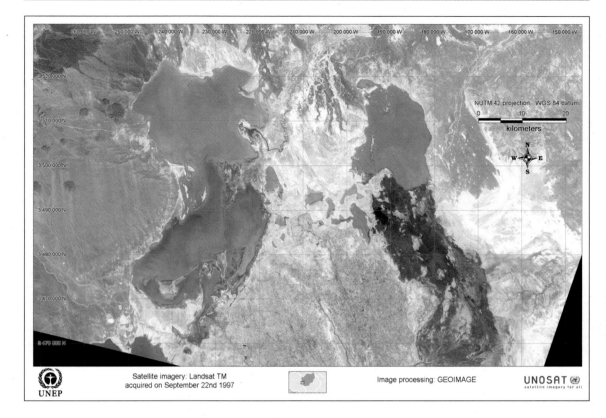

Satellite imagery: Landsat TM
acquired on September 22nd 1997

Image processing: GEOIMAGE

UNEP

UNOSAT
satellite imagery for all

➤ Satellite imagery of the Sistan basin, 2001

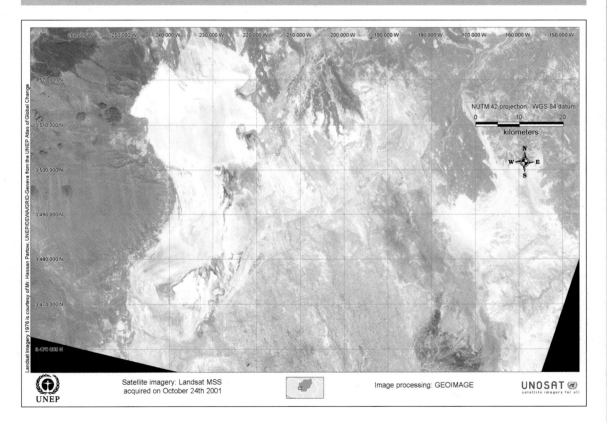

Satellite imagery: Landsat MSS
acquired on October 24th 2001

Image processing: GEOIMAGE

UNEP

UNOSAT
satellite imagery for all

AFGHANISTAN

➤ Movement of Registan sand dunes, 1986 and 2002

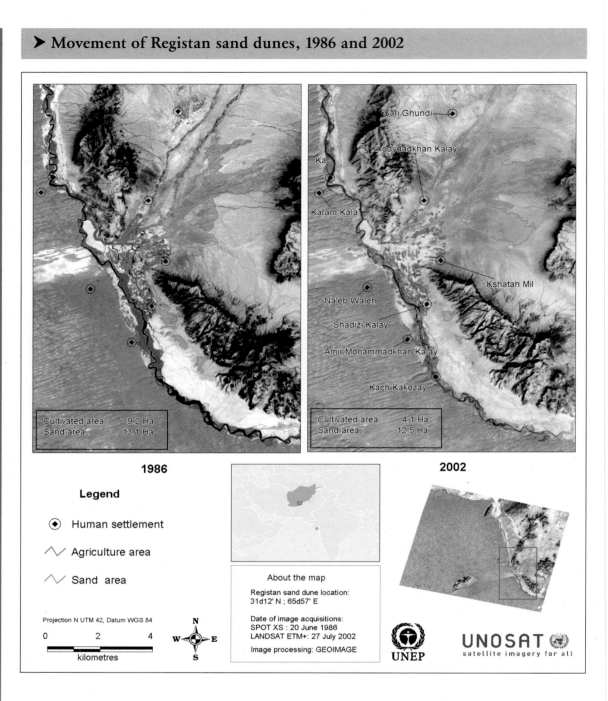

Dams and water management: UNEP estimated that together the major dams and irrigation schemes on the Helmand River have the capacity to hold at least 2.7 billion m³. UNEP was informed that both surface water and groundwater levels at many points along the Helmand dropped significantly following the period of dam construction in the 1970s. The dams were built for hydroelectricity generation and improved water distribution. However, two decades of conflict have prevented coordinated and strategic water releases. High rates of evaporation are also occurring from the surface of the reservoirs, leading to significant wastage. Finally, hydroelectric production priorities are incompatible with water release needs during periods of low precipitation. The combination of these three factors may actually have increased the vulnerability of the Sistan basin to drought rather than improved water management and distribution. Reduced annual and peak flows of the Helmand River have also reportedly resulted in decreased groundwater recharge. UNEP investigated allegations by local people that water stored at the Kajaki and Dahla dams was not released to alleviate the drought conditions in the Sistan wetlands in 2002. UNEP visited the Kajaki site and observed the water level to be 58 m out of a maximum capacity of 70 m (around 900 million m^3). Technicians reported that continuous releases of water had been made, but that these failed to reach the Sistan area due to excessive extraction en route. Small releases were also reportedly made from the Dahla dam, even through reservoir levels there were extremely low.

Increasing and uncoordinated water extraction: Throughout the entire basin UNEP either observed or was informed that water extraction has been increasing and occurring in a totally uncontrolled and unmanaged manner. One of the most serious problems involves the uncoordinated drilling of deep wells without adequate consideration given to possible impacts on existing withdrawal sites such as shallow wells, springs and the traditional *'karez'* systems – vertical shafts connecting to horizontal tunnels that extend for several kilometres underground. Millions of dollars of capital and human labour investments are being threatened by the rush to meet immediate humanitarian needs without

Spillway at Kajaki dam

considering regional impacts or long-term hydrological consequences. In one case reported by the United Nations High Commission for Refugees (UNHCR), the construction of deep wells in the Bakaw district of Farah province caused hundreds of *karez* to dry up, leading to a disruption of local livelihoods and to serious disputes over water-use rights. A second major problem identified by UNEP has been the collapse of traditional water management systems and decision-making structures at the community level. Due to the conflict, many local systems came under the direct rule of military commanders who lacked knowledge of traditional distribution rights or water infrastructure needs. Decisions were made in the best interests of each community, rather than considering the wider regional needs. As a result, many downstream users lost access to traditional supplies and disputes ensued over access to water resources.

Well drilling rig and rotation drill near Kandahar

Water-use efficiency: In Helmand province, formal irrigation schemes are estimated to account for up to 60 per cent of irrigated land. Local estimates suggest that water flowing through a large-scale formal system at a rate of 1 m^3 per second can irrigate 1 500 ha, while the same flow in *a kar*ez system can irrigate up to 10 000 ha.

AFGHANISTAN

Although production per hectare is higher from formal schemes, and *karez* systems lose significant amounts of water outside growing season, these figures suggest that the costs and benefits of formal distribution networks need further investigation to ensure the most efficient delivery of scarce water. In addition, the water-use efficiency of crops should also be assessed, as UNEP observed water-intensive crops, including watermelons, okra and cotton, being grown throughout the region despite the drought conditions.

Potential for groundwater development: UNEP collected water samples from a range of springs, *karez*, wells, rivers and public water supplies in the Helmand basin. Results indicated that the mountain-fed *karez* and rivers have low salinity values that favour irrigation and domestic use. However, these waters rapidly deteriorate in quality with distance from source, such that by the time they reach Sistan both shallow and deeper groundwaters are saline and unsuitable for either drinking or irrigation. The salinity values obtained by UNEP are comparable with samples collected in the 1970s by the Danish Committee for Aid to Afghanistan (DACAAR), indicating no significant increases in salinity in three decades. These values suggest that the potential for groundwater development in the lower reaches of the Helmand near Zaranj continues to be extremely limited.

Transboundary water management: Given that the Sistan wetlands are an important transboundary water resource, UNEP investigated current water-sharing arrangements. In 1973 an agreement was reached between Iran and Afghanistan to allow 22 m³/sec to flow into Iran from the Sistan branch of the Helmand River, located just south of Zaranj. In addition, Iran was to purchase an additional four cubic m³/sec from Afghanistan, bringing the total allocation to 26 m³/sec. While the agreement was not formally ratified by Afghanistan due to government instability, Iran constructed the Chanimeh reservoirs to store the water for drinking. The reservoirs have a capacity of 0.7 billion m³ of water and expansion to 1 billion m³ is currently being considered. In 2001 tensions between the neighbouring countries escalated when Iran wrote to the UN Secretary General, Kofi Annan, charging that the Taliban had blocked the Helmand River, causing some 140 000 ha of land in the neighbouring regions of Iran to dry up. However, a UN investigation found the drought to be the main cause, as the Helmand River was flowing at only 2 per cent of its annual average . In 2002 UNEP was informed that the lower reaches of the Helmand had experienced significant flows for 40 days in spring 2002. However, accusations have been made by local Afghan farmers that none of this water got past the Chanimeh diversion, leading to significant water shortages north of Zaranj, including in the Sistan basin. Nevertheless, Iran has again accused Afghanistan of not honouring the water-sharing agreement.

In a gesture of goodwill, waters were released from the Kajaki dam on 25 October 2002. However, the flow stopped ten days later. High-level discussions to resolve the dispute are ongoing between the two countries.

RENE NIJENHUIS/UNEP, 2002

Sample of silt taken for pesticide analysis from Zaranj

Pesticide residues: Samples of silt from Zaranj and sediments from the dried-up reed swamp north of Zaranj and the Helmand riverbed were analysed for pesticide residues. The analyses detected very low levels

Post-Conflict Environmental Assessment

(0.02 mg/kg) of Dieldrin, a highly toxic organochlorine pesticide used in insect control. Dieldrin has been banned in many countries for over 20 years, but stocks are likely to have been used in Afghanistan until recently, and possibly may continue to be used. Although the level of Dieldrin recorded was low, it is significant as it can be absorbed by aquatic organisms and eventually enter the human food chain. A level of 0.02 mg/kg will take up to 50 years to degrade. Its accumulation in the reed swamp suggests that it made its way into the basin via the Helmand or Farah River systems. Further studies are needed to properly assess the distribution, quantities and risks of Dieldrin in the Sistan lakes area.

New diversion schemes: UNEP was informed of a scheme by the Ministry of Irrigation, Water Resources and Environment to re-establish the Kamal Khan Flood Control project in the lower Helmand basin. The project came to a stop during the conflicts. Its purpose is to divert excess floodwaters to the Gaud-e-Zireh depression. In addition this project aims to regulate irrigation water for Afghanistan and Iran, while at the same time maintaining sustainable water levels in the Hamoun-i-Puzak and Hamoun-i-Sabiri lakes. Further studies are needed to determine if these twin goals can be achieved.

ANTHONY FITZHERBERT/UNEP, 2002.

Headwaters of the Amu Darya River

Amu Darya basin

The Amu Darya River flows into the north of Afghanistan and forms the border with Tajikistan, Uzbekistan and Turkmenistan. The entire basin is estimated to cover 227 800 km², of which approximately 39 per cent lies in Afghanistan[54]. Sub-catchments in the Afghan provinces of Badakhshan, Takhar, Baghlan, Konduz, Balkh and Jowzjan contribute to the flow. In ancient times the Amu Darya was called the Oxus and figured importantly in the history of Persia and in the campaigns of Alexander the Great.

The two primary headwaters of the Amu Darya River originate in the high peaks of the Pamir mountains in the Wakhan Corridor. The northern branch, the Pamir River, has its source in Zor Kul Lake, which is shared by Tajikistan and Afghanistan. The southern branch, the Wakhan River, flows out of Chakmatin Lake.

Less than 20 years ago the course of the river ran for 1 200 km before emptying into the Aral Sea. Today the river dries up before reaching the Aral Sea due to excessive extraction of its waters for cotton and hydroelectric production in the bordering central Asian republics. This has been a major factor in the decreased surface area of the Aral Sea, from 68 000 km^2 to 28 700 km^2, and to decreases in volume from 1 040 km^3 to only 181 km^3 [55].

In addition to its transboundary significance, the Amu Darya River and its tributaries are also a critical source of water supply for the extensive irrigated areas in Afghanistan's northern fertile plains. About 40 per cent of the country's irrigated lands lie in this northern region[56].

Given the national and transboundary importance of this resource, UNEP visited the provinces of Balkh and Jawzjan to assess the prevailing environmental conditions. Information was collected on water quality, key threats and pressures, and on possible future plans for water extraction for either irrigation or hydroelectric development. The status of transboundary agreements was also investigated.

Key findings:

Locust control and pesticides: Infestations of Moroccan locust (*Dociostaurus maroccanus*) occur annually in northern Afghanistan. The scale and intensity of the infestations vary from year to year. In 2001 aid workers reported that more than half the agricultural land was infested in some of the northern provinces. This was due to dry weather conditions and inadequate prevention, but also because agricultural fields had been extended to the edge of the desert, near areas already infested by locusts[57]. While manual labour is the preferred method for combating such infestations, pesticides are often used when manual techniques are overwhelmed by the size of the outbreak. For example, in 2002 five vehicle-mounted and 1 300 hand-held sprayers were used to apply almost 30 000 litres of pesticides[58].

UNEP was unable to assess the potential environmental risks from the pesticide as spraying operations had been completed by the time of the assessment. However, large stocks of dangerous or illegal pesticides are reported to exist from previous control efforts. According to recent surveys conducted by GOAL, an Irish NGO working in the area, the pesticide methyl-parathion is widely available at the bazaar in Mazar-e-Sharif for around US$5 per bottle. Under certain exposure conditions, methyl-parathion can affect the central nervous

UNEP expert conducting interviews with local people in Aqchah

RENE NIJENHUIS/UNEP, 2002

RENE NIJENHUIS/UNEP, 2002

Sand dune moving across main road near Mazar-e-Sharif

system, resulting in dizziness, headaches, breathing difficulties, vomiting, diarrhoea, tremors, blurred vision, sweating, and possibly death. A previous assessment conducted by IUCN in 1991[59] reported nearly 7 000 metric tonnes of the persistent, toxic and carcinogenic pesticide BHC (benzene hexachloride, also known as Lindane) were being stored at sites in Mazar-e-Sharif, Pul-i-Khomri, Aibak, Kunduz and Khulum. No information was available to UNEP on the current location or storage condition of these sites. However, UNEP learned that there is virtually no management of hazardous chemicals in Afghanistan. Nor is there any monitoring of pesticide residues in humans or in the environment. Positive steps are, however, being taken by FAO toward the use of integrated pest management (IPM) in order to reduce possible human and environmental health impacts. Preparations are under way for the 2003 locust control campaign, during which 60 000 ha will be sprayed, with mechanical control measures on a further 100 000 ha[60].

Sand dunes and erosion: The sand dune belt lies south of the Amu Darya, measuring over 300 km long and up to 30 km wide. In Balkh province the dunes rise to a height of 15 m and cross the main road to the Bridge of Friendship over a 12-km zone. UNEP observed that sand dunes are moving onto agricultural land in the small alluvial strip next to the Amu Darya, as well as into human settlements. Increased dune movement has occurred in recent years due to the loss of stabilizing vegetation, much of which has died and been harvested for fuel. Along the main road towards the Bridge of Friendship the dunes move up to one metre per day in moderate winds, in an east–west direction. The moving sand frequently blocks roads, forcing people to establish new routes, in some cases through mined areas. Compounding the problem, natural barriers to the sand have vanished with the loss of tree cover from around villages and from riparian areas. Extensive erosion of riverbanks, leading to siltation and the loss of valuable farmland, is also on the increase due to the loss of tree roots holding the soil in place.

Hydro development: The total hydroelectric potential of the entire Amu Darya River amounts to 306 billion kilowatt hours[61]. It is reported that to date only 10 per cent of the hydroelectric potential of the Amu Darya in Afghanistan has been developed. Most of the potential

AFGHANISTAN

lies in the upstream region of the river, in particular its tributaries. According to the Ministry of Water and Power, approximately 96 per cent of the country's future energy needs will come from hydroelectric development. However, the basis for future development was drawn up in 1980, and it does not adequately take into account water needs during drought conditions or transboundary needs and agreements. Furthermore, it does not reflect the recommendations of the World Bank's World Commission on Dams report[62]. A major over-haul of the planning base is urgently needed.

Gas pipelines for irrigation: UNEP was informed of plans to use an abandoned gas pipe-line for future irrigation purposes. The existing pipeline runs from Shebergan to Uzbekistan and crosses the Amu Darya close to the border with Turkmenistan. Water from the Amu Darya would be abstracted and exported to the Aqchah plains. No precise details could be obtained on the status of this project, but an increase in abstraction could have important regional implications for the downstream countries.

Groundwater salinity: UNEP conducted limited sampling of groundwater salinity levels in Aqchah and found the groundwater in this area to be saline and often at a fairly shallow depth. For example, in the town of Aqchah the electrical conductivity (EC – a measure of salinity) is 4 010 mS/cm at a stated depth of 25 m. FAO guidelines classify any values above EC 3 000 mS/cm as severe salinity and unsuitable for irrigation. Further north, the water table appears to shallow quite rapidly but is still heavily saline. Samples taken from wells outside the town of Aqchah, at depths of 10 and 13 m, revealed EC values of 4 070 mS/cm and 3 280 mS/cm respectively. In contrast to these values, surface water salinity from the Balkh River irrigation scheme was 1 030 mS/cm, while a sample taken from the Amu Darya was 587 mS/cm.

Transboundary cooperation: Movement toward transboundary cooperation over the management of the Amu Darya began in the 1940s. Two important agreements eventually established the current framework for cooperation: the 1946 *Frontier Agreement between Afghanistan and the USSR*, and the 1958 *Treaty concerning the regime to the Soviet-Afghan frontier*, including the *Protocol concerning the joint execution of works for the integrated utilization of the water resources in the frontier section of the Amu Darya.* These agreements established an international commission to deal with the use and quality of frontier water resources. After the collapse of the Soviet Union, the central Asian republics of Tajikistan, Uzbekistan and Turkmenistan inherited the responsibilities of this commission. Afghanistan was not, however, able to make any substantial contributions or commitments on transboundary resources during the period of conflict. Even without the cooperation of Afghanistan, the five central Asian republics have recognized the urgent need to cooperate on water issues. A number of initiatives, including the Interstate Commission for Water Management Coordination (ICWC) and the International Fund for the Aral Sea (IFAS), have been created to conduct transboundary water management. The United Nations Economic Commission for Europe (UNECE) has also established the Special Programme for the Economies of Central Asia (SPECA) to strengthen cooperation between countries and explore transboundary resource management options. To date, Afghanistan, a fundamental partner to any future transboundary water management agreement, has not participated in any of the discussions.

Band-e-Amir Lakes and the wetlands of Kole Hashmat Khan, Dasht-e-Nawar and Ab-e-Estada

The Band-e-Amir Lakes and the wetlands of Kole Hashmat Khan, Dasht-e-Nawar and Ab-e-Estada were also assessed to determine their current hydrological status. As each of these areas is also a protected area, a description of each site, as well as UNEP's findings are located in the protected areas section on page 73.

■ Forest and woodland

Forests and wooded lands are particularly valuable in dry land regions such as Afghanistan. They provide fuelwood and timber, the latter with major export potential, as well as other forest products such as nuts and medicinal plants. Forests are also prime habitat for many animal species, including some threatened with extinction. Extensive tree cover can also help to moderate local climate conditions and reduce potentially damaging runoff after sudden rainfall. In many situations, water courses in forested land will retain their dry-season flows better than those in unforested land, making water available for human consumption and irrigation during critical periods.

There are generally three distinct types of tree cover in Afghanistan: forests of mixed oak and conifers, open woodlands, and riparian forest. Tree cover tends naturally to be more continuous along the eastern border with Pakistan, where precipitation is far higher than elsewhere, more evenly distributed through the year and less erratic. The mixed oak and coniferous forests of the east have potential to be managed as sources of timber, but are now being logged illegally, severely reducing the country's natural resource base. Over most of the centre and north of the country, conditions for tree growth are more marginal, and existing tree cover is extremely sensitive to disturbances that may then lead to erosion and desertification. In these regions, open woodlands, with pistachio and almond, are valuable sources of nuts for subsistence and export, but have been increasingly cut for fuelwood.

Overgrazing combined with an increasing population and corresponding demands for fuelwood over recent decades have resulted in extensive decline in these woodlands. In the Amu Darya plains and the southwest arid zones, tree growth is mainly limited to narrow strips of 'tugai' forest, riparian woodland and scrubby vegetation, dominated by poplar, willow and tamarisk, that occurs in the often relatively narrow transition zone between open water and adjacent desert or semi-desert. These forests provide important sources of fuelwood and timber for construction as well as critical wildlife habitat. They also promote riverbank stability.

Forest cover is generally believed to have been far more extensive prior to human occupation of the country. Despite the pressure on natural resources generated by competing empires, historical sources suggest that substantial forests, as well as more continuous open woodland, remained in many parts well into the Mughal period, which dates back to the

AREA, 2002

Conifer forests in Nangarhar province

AFGHANISTAN

first half of the 16th century. Assessing the incomplete evidence available to them in the late 1970s, FAO concluded that most of north, central and eastern Afghanistan was wooded until early in the 19th century[63]. At the time of their report, however, forest loss appeared to be more rapid than ever before, with the mounting need for fuelwood and the impacts of livestock on tree survival and regeneration the driving factors.

Estimates at that time suggested that almost 1 million ha of oak forest existed, and about 2 million hectares of coniferous forest, mainly pine and cedar. In total these forests amounted to some 4.5 per cent of the land area. Only in some relatively restricted areas in the east, primarily in Kunar and Nuristan provinces, was forest area and condition considered good enough to provide a potential basis for commercial forestry. In addition to these relatively closed forests, various types of open woodland, with pistachio, juniper and other species, covered about 32 million ha, or 48 per cent of the land area[64].

An important objective of UNEP's assessment, apart from reassessing the state of Afghanistan's woodlands and forests after the years of recent conflict, was to identify steps toward effective management of these resources so they can continue to sustain rural livelihoods as well as biodiversity and ecosystem processes. UNEP studied sites within the northern pistachio-juniper zone, areas of conifer forest in the east, and *tugai* forests along the Amu Darya.

Open woodland

Open woodland with pistachio was probably once widespread at low and medium elevations on the slopes of the Hindu Kush. In recent times, Badghis province in northwest Afghanistan has held the most continuous and productive pistachio woodlands, but patches of this vegetation type remain widely distributed in a zone along the northern slopes and foothills of the Hindu Kush, eastward to Takhar and Badakhshan. Above 1 500 m pistachio is increasingly replaced by juniper. In an essentially arid country, these woodlands are an important element in the livelihood of local people, providing nuts, fuelwood and a source of grazing for livestock. Given the evidence for widespread decline, it will be important in developing management policy to emphasize uses that have low impact and high value, such as pistachio harvesting. It will also be necessary to seek alternatives to damaging practices such as fuelwood collection. A variety of measures have been implemented locally, aiming to manage the collection of pistachio nuts and limit wood cutting, but there is considerable need for such measures to be developed and employed more widely.

These woodlands are also key to maintaining biological diversity. Dead wood, leaf and other litter, and herbaceous ground cover support a rich diversity of invertebrates, and these in turn support a variety of birds and small mammals. They also enrich the soil, promoting grass growth for grazing. Tree roots help stabilize soil and leaves lessen the impact of rainfall, reducing erosion.

Key findings:

Pistachio deforestation: UNEP visited the provinces of Herat, Badghis, Kunduz and Takhar to survey pistachio deforestation. Pistachio woodlands were observed near the villages of Farkhar, Qala-i-Nau, Narop, and Kushka Kuhna, in stands averaging 20–40 trees per hectare. However, in the majority of surveyed areas, UNEP observed vast landscapes of bare or eroding soil where dense woodlands of pistachio once stood less than 30 years ago. Forest officers in Badghis and Takhar provinces indicated that 50–70 per cent of pistachio woodland cover had been lost over the past three decades. UNEP conducted satellite-image analyses in both provinces to determine how the distribution of woodlands had changed between 1977 and 2002. In 1977 woodlands were detected on 55 per cent of the land base in Badghis and on 37 per cent in Takhar. The density of woodlands ranged from 40 to 100 trees per hectare. In 2002 the density of woodlands had decreased in both provinces to the point where they could no longer be detected by satellite instruments. This either suggests complete deforestation, or a reduction in density to less than 40 trees per hectare. This finding is consistent with field observations, although additional ground verification is required. Much of the loss was reported to have been caused in the uncertain political conditions following the Soviet occupation. During this period residents reportedly stockpiled large amounts of fuelwood, as future access to these lands was perceived to be threatened. During subsequent conflicts, military forces also cut trees for fuelwood and to reduce hiding and ambush

Kushkahkunah region

Kushkahkunah region

Qala-i-Nau region

Qala-i-Nau region

Farkhar region

Pistachio woodlands in Afghanistan have suffered extensive deforestation. Left-hand photos show intact but degraded pistachio woodlands. Right-hand photos show complete deforestation.

Farkhar region

> **Woodland cover change, Takhar and Kunduz provinces, 1977 and 2002**

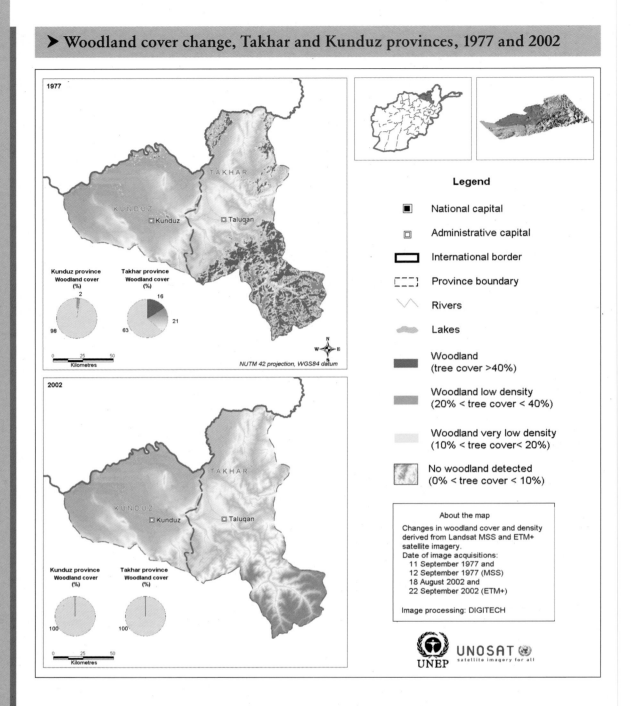

opportunities for opposing forces. Deforestation has since continued, with fuelwood demand increasing due to population growth. An "Afghan Conservation Corps" has been proposed as one of the key tools for conducting reforestation of degraded areas. The joint proposal by the US Government and the Afghan Transitional Authority is a labour intensive project designed to provide immediate employment benefits to vulnerable people and ex-combatants, while at the same time contributing to forest restoration at 18 locations across the country.

Fuel demand: Information gathered by UNEP in Badghis province suggests that woody shrubs and dried dung meet about 50 per cent of a family's fuel needs for the year in that region, while pistachio wood provides the other half. This amounts to 2 000–4 000 kg of pistachio wood per year, approximately equivalent to 20–40 trees per family annually (given about 100 kg per tree). While a rigorous assessment of the amounts actually involved is still needed, these calculations indicate the magnitude of use and the role of pistachio woodland in local livelihoods. It is not clear at present to what extent fuelwood is obtained

➤ **Woodland cover change, Badghis province, 1977 and 2002**

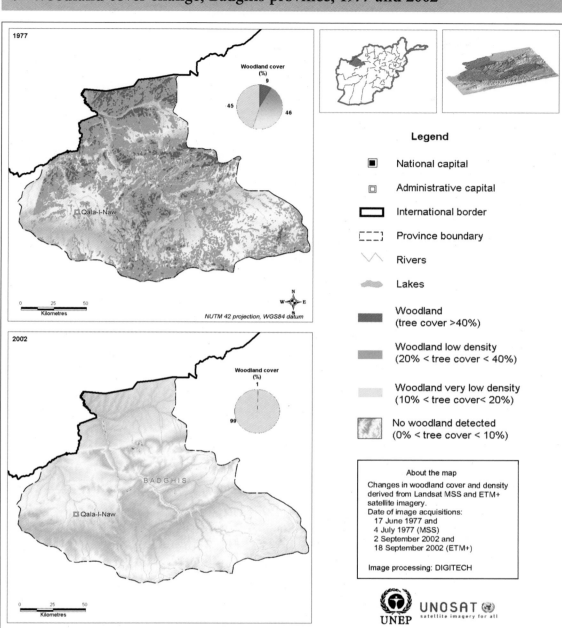

by removing individual branches or by felling entire trees. All the mature trees observed by UNEP showed evidence of limb removal, followed by regrowth. This confirms that an as yet unknown level of branch harvesting is potentially sustainable. However, UNEP also observed that entire trees, including their root systems, are removed for fuelwood and when land is converted for dry land cultivation.

Natural regeneration: Virtually no live seedlings were found during UNEP field visits. This is likely to be caused by two factors. First, all pistachio woodland areas visited and observed by UNEP were used for grazing domestic livestock, primarily sheep and goats. While conflict and drought have reduced livestock populations, observed flocks consisted of 200–300 animals on average. However, no rotation or other regulation of grazing appears to be used. The second possible contributing factor is that pistachio nuts are collected locally and provide a valuable export commodity. Local residents reported that a mature tree may produce 35–50 kg of nuts per year, for which local collectors can receive up to

US$1 per kilogram (with shells). An average family in one village reportedly collects about 160 kg annually, a substantial part of their income, while around Farkhar village (in Takhar) nuts worth more than US$25 000 were collected during 2002. The high monetary value of pistachio nuts means that virtually every single nut on the tree, or falling to the ground, is collected, with an obvious impact on the potential for woodland regeneration.

Afghans harvesting pistachio branches for fuelwood

Erosion and flooding: The combination of drought and heavy grazing pressure has caused the gradual loss of other vegetation cover, leaving the soil vulnerable to erosion by water and wind. Residents report that this condition has increased the rate of run-off and the frequency of flooding. The problem is further compounded by the removal of riparian vegetation. Without roots to anchor soils to the

Livestock grazing in pistachio forests near Narop

riverbank, flood events lead to significant bank erosion and loss of agricultural land. UNEP investigated this phenomenon in the Cheshmaduzduk River valley, near Qala-i-Nau. At one location where the channel once averaged 50 m in width, it now extends to 250 m (a 5-fold increase). Hundreds of hectares of agricultural lands have also been washed down the river as a consequence of the erosion.

Drought impacts: The recent drought has led to the death of some branches, but little tree mortality. However, the availability of dead branches appears to have increased the amount of fuelwood harvested. Pistachio nut harvests have been reduced by up to 50 per cent during recent drought years.

Bank erosion in Cheshmanduzuk River valley, near Qala-i-Nau

Local management: Forest management regulations were enacted by the central and local governments in the 1970s. The laws prohibited cutting, grazing or cultivating in pistachio forests without permission. Living within a pistachio forest was also illegal. The laws were enforced by local forest wardens in each of the districts and the system was managed by district forest

Post-Conflict Environmental Assessment

MARTYN MURRAY/UNEP,2002

300-year-old sacred pistachio tree protected by local communities near Narop

offices of the Ministry of Agriculture. A local management system for harvesting pistachio nuts, known as the '*shule*', was also developed. However, after 1979, and throughout the 1980s and 1990s, the systems broke down, leaving a management void and an opportunity for uncontrolled exploitation. While some communities, such as the village of Farkhar, independently hired forest wardens to enforce the *shule* and prevent illegal cutting, it is reported that most communities did not take such measures. With the gradual breakdown of government control, and with increasing economic and political insecurity, grazing, dry land cultivation, and timber harvesting in pistachio areas accelerated, and large-scale deforestation reportedly followed.

MARTYN MURRAY/UNEP,2002

Juniper forests of Subzac pass

Juniper woodland: Little new information on Afghanistan's juniper woodland is available and UNEP had difficulty locating existing accessible stands. The only juniper woodland that could be visited by UNEP was in the Subzac pass, in Herat province. It was estimated that 50 per cent of the juniper cover in the Subzac pass has been lost in the last 30 years. Local sources at Kushka Kuhna in Badghis province confirmed that as much as 80 per cent of juniper woodland had been cut during the past two decades. Where it once grew in belts adjacent to pistachio woods, only isolated pockets now remain. As juniper is used for roofing timber as well as fuelwood, cutting often entails removal of the entire tree. It was reported that grazing is also occurring throughout many juniper woodlands, possibly preventing successful regeneration.

NATURAL RESOURCES

AFGHANISTAN

Oak and conifer forests

Tree cover and composition of oak and coniferous forests in Afghanistan's mountainous eastern provinces, adjacent to Pakistan, vary with elevation and the amount of monsoon rainfall that reaches the area from the Indian subcontinent. In the forests at lower elevations, the main pine and cedar belt lies between 2 500 and 3 300 m. This tends to be replaced by juniper at higher elevations, giving way to alpine meadows and the snowline. The mountains of eastern Afghanistan hold a rich fauna, including snow leopard, markhor, Asian ibex (*Capra sibirica*) and urial. Among many forest species are Himalayan black bear

Cedar logging in Kunar province

(*Ursus thibetanus*) and two species of flying squirrel (*Eoglaucomys fimbriatus* and *Petaurista petaurista*). There is also a rich diversity of birds. Hunting is a strong local tradition, and there is potential for commercial sport hunting if local hunting can be controlled and existing populations of wild goat and sheep are maintained or increased to sustainable levels.

Deodar cedar (*Cedrus deodara*) in particular has been harvested in commercial quantities from these mountains for several decades. In Kunar and Nuristan, logging greatly increased in the 1960s and 1970s, and subsequent attempts to regulate timber extraction have proved ineffective. A 1993 estimate by FAO[65] suggested that forest cover in the east had decreased by 16 per cent to about 12 000 km² since the 1970s, a loss of some 2 300 km². The apparent rapid decline in forest cover made visiting Kunar and Nuristan a top priority for UNEP. However site visits were not possible because of a deterioration in the security situation. Efforts were redirected to consultation with officials and other personnel, surveys of timber markets, and a visit to a community forestry and tree nursery project in Nangarhar province.

Key findings:

Forest cover: The amount of forest cover that has been lost in the last two decades is estimated by officials to be 30 per cent. However, local forest officers and some residents describe this number as conservative, and suggest the true figure lies between 50 and 70 per cent. To confirm these estimates, UNEP obtained Landsat satellite images covering the provinces of Nuristan, Kunar and Nangarhar for 1977 and 2002. The analyses revealed that forest cover has decreased by a total of 52 per cent when the provinces are taken together. Individually, Nangarhar province

Cedar beams hauled by mule, Kunar province

➤ Forest cover change, Nuristan, Kunar and Nangarhar provinces, 1977 and 2002

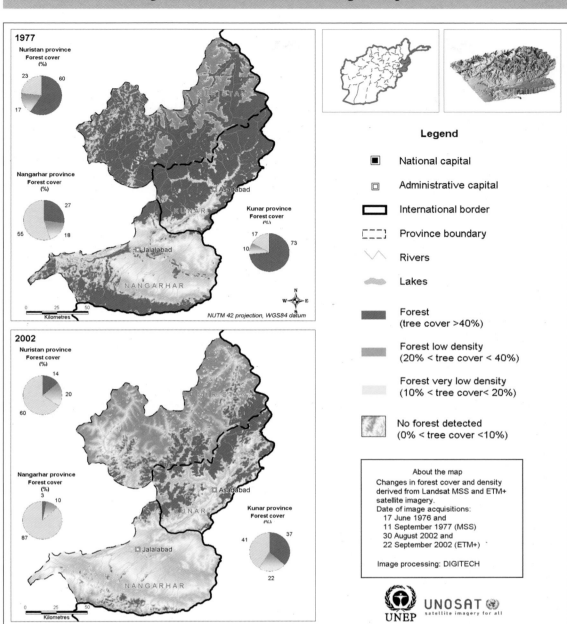

has been the hardest hit, with a 71 per cent decrease in forest cover. Meanwhile, forest cover in Nuristan has decreased by 53 per cent, and Kunar by 29 per cent. Residents predict similar losses for the forested regions in the provinces of Paktya, Khost and Paktika.

Commercial timber extraction: Deodar cedar is the primary conifer species harvested. It is a straight-grained, decay-resistant, aromatic wood. High grades are used for furniture, cabinet-making, doors and window frames. Lesser grades are used for house and bridge construction. The properties of the wood and the diversity of applications generate a high demand both within Afghanistan, as well as from external sources such as Pakistan and the Near East. During Mujahadeen and Taliban times, local government officers reported that up to 200 timber trucks could be observed per day on the main road in Kunar province. As each truck can carry a volume of timber representing five to ten trees (44 cubic metres), this represents an offtake of up to 200 ha per day from the Kunar and Nuristan region (assuming a density of 20 mature trees per hectare). Although the Transitional Authority has issued a timber ban to stop the uncontrolled logging of the resource, an average of 25

AFGHANISTAN

to 50 trucks can still be seen per day on the main Kunar roads. It is reported that thousands of local people depend on the forest sector to earn their living. Cedar trees are typically cut into beams measuring 15 cm deep by 30 cm wide by 2.5 metres long (0.11 cubic metres per beam). Local communities obtain between US$3-5 dollars per beam. The same beam can be sold for US$50 in Afghan markets and up to US$85 in Pakistan. Due to the high prices in Pakistan, local timber yards reported that for every 15 trucks of timber that transit through Jalalabad, 10 go to Pakistan, 3 continue to Kabul, and 2 remain in Jalalabad for local consumption. If this division is reflective of the regional situation, export markets in Pakistan could account for approximately 66 per cent of the timber cut.

Forest ownership: A large proportion of the population in the eastern provinces depends on the forest sector economically. However, many local communities have lost control over their resources and forests are being consumed for immediate profit by a very small minority. Warlords, 'timber barons' and traders from other countries have sought to make windfall profits from current export opportunities. Such profits are potentially very high. This needs to be addressed so that the country as a whole benefits from sustainable forest use. The Ministry of Agriculture and Animal Husbandry has proposed to establish a "Green Force" in order to prevent illegal timber harvesting of conifer forests. An "Afghan Conservation Corps" has also been proposed as one of the key tools for conducting reforestation of degraded areas. The joint proposal by the US Government and the Afghan Transitional Authority is a labour intensive project designed to provide immediate employment benefits to vulnerable people and ex-combatents, while at the same time contributing to forest restoration at 18 locations across the country.

Road building: Road building is reported to have increased access to forested areas, facilitating significant deforestation. There are no policies in place to restrict access, and road building is conducted in an uncoordinated way.

Reconstruction needs: Increased demand for high-quality timber to meet reconstruction needs could increase domestic prices and lead to additional harvesting pressures. To date, no measures have been taken to coordinate timber procurement from national and regional

MARTYN MURRAY/UNEP.2002

Trucks loaded with cedar beams for export to Pakistan

Post-Conflict Environmental Assessment

sources in order to supply reconstruction needs in a sustainable manner. The United Nations High Commissioner for Refugees (UNHCR) currently imports the majority of timber used for shelter construction from South African sources due to a lack of domestic supply. UNHCR recognizes the immediate need to undertake a systematic analysis of local and regional timber supply sources.

Wildlife: It was reported by local people and market vendors that the forested valleys of the eastern provinces, in particular Kunar and Nuristan, still contain markhor, urial and Asiatic black bear. However, UNEP could not confirm this report, due to access restrictions.

Tugai forests

UNEP also visited *tugai* forest islands in the Amu Darya near Imam Sahib. As the location visited is also proposed as a protected area, a description of the site, as well as UNEP's findings are located in the following section on page 83.

■ Protected areas

Protected areas were first introduced in the West primarily as a means to protect landscapes, wildlife and habitats of particular value, often by exclusion of people and regulation of access and use. More modern approaches stress the need for community participation in protected area planning, and for multiple uses aimed to benefit residents as well as maintain natural processes. Evidence from around the world shows that with suitable design and management these twin goals can be achieved.

Since the 1970s, there has been greater recognition of the cultural, aesthetic, recreational and economic significance of the need to protect forests, wetlands and other habitats rich in biological diversity. To work effectively, protected areas must provide economic and social benefits and involve local people in management as partners and decision-makers. In addition, the most effective protected areas are those linked by corridors, protected by buffer zones and designed to maximize resilience to threats.

Afghanistan has never had the benefit of an effective protected areas system. Although some progress was made in implementing a protected areas network designed during the 1970s[66], the escalation of disorder through that decade, and the Soviet occupation in 1979, prevented its development and modernization.

In Mughal times, five hundred years ago, specified areas were set aside as hunting grounds. More recently, in the 1970s, a small number of sites were similarly used by the former royal family, having been declared by royal decree as waterfowl sanctuaries or wildlife reserves. A 1992 government review listed the existing protected areas as one national park (Band-e-Amir), three waterfowl sanctuaries (Ab-i-Estada, Dasht-e-Nawar and Kole Hashmat Khan) and two wildlife reserves (Ajar Valley and Pamir-i-Buzurg). Between 1977 and 1992 a further ten sites were proposed for protected area status, including three important areas in the western half of the country: Registan Desert Wildlife Management Reserve, Hamun-i-Puzak Waterfowl Sanctuary, and Northwest Afghanistan Game Management Reserve. However, there has never been an overall enabling legislation providing for the establishment and management of protected areas, and the precise current legal status of each protected area is uncertain. Most were never formally gazetted and institutional structures have since changed. Afghanistan is not yet party to the Ramsar Convention, though several wetland sites in the country have previously been identified as of international importance for migratory and breeding waterbirds. In addition, despite some of the rich biodiversity contained within the country, a comprehensive assessment of biodiversity has never been conducted.

➤ Existing and proposed protected areas in Afghanistan

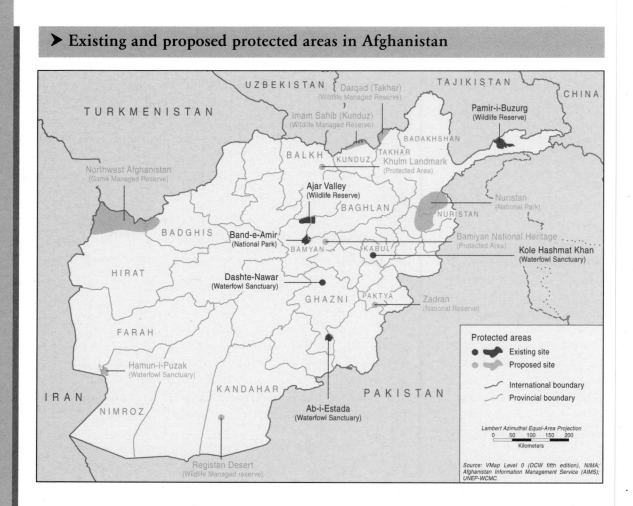

UNEP aimed to gather information from the designated protected areas in the east-centre of the country, including Band-e-Amir, Ab-i-Estada, Dasht-e-Nawar and Kole Hashmat Khan. The *tugai* forest islands of Imam Sahib were also observed from the banks of the Amu Darya. Other sections of this report also detail findings from assessments to the Pamir-e-Buzurg Wildlife Reserve and the proposed Hamoun-i-Puzak Waterfowl Sanctuary. Besides making an assessment of the status of these sites, particularly with regard to the effects of conflict and drought, a principal objective was to identify options for future management, seeking to support the twin goals of local development and maintenance of biodiversity. The Ajar Valley Wildlife Reserve and potential forested sites in Nuristan could not be accessed because of recent local disorder.

Band-e-Amir National Park

Band-e-Amir's six lakes of crystal-clear water, separated by white travertine dams and surrounded by spectacular red cliffs, comprise one of the world's uniquely beautiful natural landscapes. The lakes lie in an east-west trending valley at approximately 2 900 m elevation. From west to east the lakes are Gholaman, Qambar, Haibat, Panir, Pudina, and Zulfiqar. The travertine dams separating the lakes form when gaseous carbon dioxide from calcium-rich spring water is driven out by bacterial or algal activity, forming the mineral deposits that create the dams. While travertine dammed lakes are found in other locations (such as Fossil Creek in Arizona, United States, and Plitvice Lakes in Croatia), Band-e-Amir is a particularly striking example of the phenomenon. The lakes have attracted local and foreign tourists for many decades, and the site became Afghanistan's first national park in 1973. The site also contains a shrine dedicated to the Caliph Ali, the son-in-law and cousin of the Prophet Mohammad.

Post-Conflict Environmental Assessment

Key findings:

Band-e-Amir National Park

Hydrological condition: UNEP found the Band-e-Amir lakes to be in good hydrological condition and generally unchanged since studies conducted in 1977 by FAO and UNDP[67]. Water levels in the lakes were high, despite the worst drought in living memory. Water clarity was excellent and pH values averaged 7.0. The travertine dams appear to be intact and the vegetation is little changed. This is vividly depicted in repeat photographs taken in 1977 and 2002, although at different seasons of the year.

Protected area status: The site was declared a national park in 1973 in response to a petition from the Afghan Tourist Organization (ATO). However, the declaration was never published in the official government gazette by the Ministry of Justice and, therefore, has no legal status. A strategy for the establishment and development of the park was developed by FAO in 1977, but never implemented[68]. The President of the ATO indicated that

➤ Band-e-Amir National Park

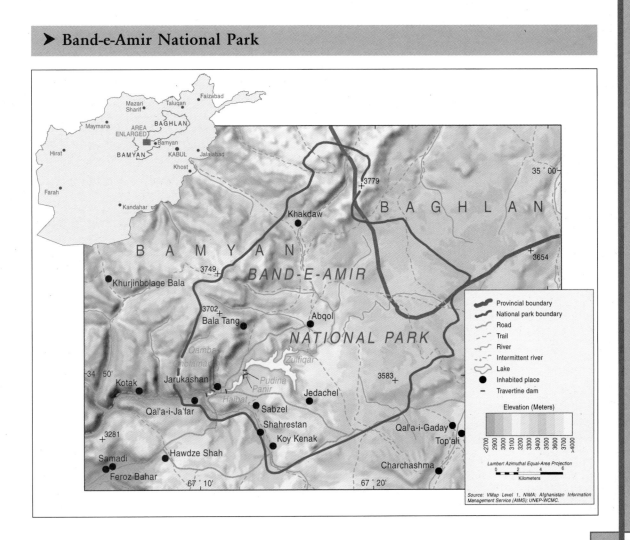

AFGHANISTAN

Band-e-Amir is a central component of the ATO's tourism strategy and that local people will benefit from tourism in the park. Band-e-Amir is also recognized as containing a unique combination of features that meet formal criteria for acceptance as a UNESCO World Heritage Natural Site. Since the Transitional Authority intends to start with a clean legislative slate, the opportunity exists to institute Band-e-Amir as a national park with legislation that reflects current best practices in park management while recognizing and accommodating historical tradition and local needs.

Photographs repeated from the same location at Band-e-Amir in 1977 and 2002

Tourism impacts: Impacts from current tourism activity included fishing with explosive devices such as guns and rockets, and erosion of the travertine slopes by vehicles. UNEP also observed that initial signs of water pollution (for example, debris in the lake, build-up of green algae) are appearing around the shrine. People were also observed throwing paper, plastic, melon rinds, and the body parts of slaughtered animals into the lake.

War impacts: Band-e-Amir was one of the front lines for fighting between Taliban and resistance forces during much of 2001. Consequently, the area is heavily mined. The direct road from Bamiyan to Band-e-Amir has not been cleared and was the location of a tragic incident in July 2002 in which a passenger bus hit an anti-tank mine with the loss of 13 lives. The entire south shore of the lake system was also considered too dangerous for UNEP to access. Clearing mines is an obvious prerequisite to developing a tourist industry and protecting wildlife at the site.

Human settlement: The four main villages located around the park, including Jaru Kashan, Qela Jafar, Dew Khana and Kupruk, have a total estimated population of between 2 000 and 2 500. Local people interviewed by UNEP indicated that they benefited from tourism prior to the war. Residents and community leaders had a mainly positive attitude toward

Local tourism at Band-e-Amir

Post-Conflict Environmental Assessment

full establishment of national park status, providing the financial benefits are equally distributed between the villages.

Wildlife: UNEP was informed that hunting of urial and ibex is occurring in the area, primarily north of Band-e-Amir at Pudinatu, Siakhol, Seratour, Sardeega and Cheshma Lashkar. Populations of these species have declined dramatically, although animals are seen occasionally within 2 km of Band-e-Amir at Seena Boloq (near Balatang). Most of the hunters are military men and their activities are deeply resented by local residents. Those interviewed indicated that they would like to see the government control hunting.

Kole Hashmat Khan Waterfowl Sanctuary

Kole Hashmat Khan is a shallow, reed-covered lake situated at the edge of the metropolis of Kabul. It was long used as a royal hunting area and was declared as a waterfowl reserve in the 1930s by King Zahir Shah. The site has great recreational value for the residents of Kabul and is important for migrating and wintering waterbirds and as a source of reeds for roofing thatch. The area around Kole Hashmat Khan contains many historical sites, including Latif's Garden, formerly located to the northwest of the lake; the shrine of Jabur Ansar, built in 645 AD; and the Jabar Ansar Wali Cemetery. To the northwest lies the imposing fort of Bala Hissar, overlooking the lake from a high hill.

Ditch dug around Kole Hashmat Khan

PETER ZAHLER/UNEP, 2002

Key findings:

Hydrological condition: No areas of open water were visible in summer 2002, although the lake had reportedly been half-a-metre deep in spring. The environmental change at the wetland is clearly depicted in repeat photographs taken in 1977 and 2002. Reportedly, water levels were last normal in 1998. Current desiccation is being caused by the drought and by increasing diversion of water away from water courses feeding the lake. The Kamari canal is a first priority for water allocation, followed by the Shewaki canal. UNEP also observed that an 8-km ditch had been dug completely around Kole Hashmat Khan as a means of delineating the boundaries and keeping livestock out. While the intention may be well meant, the ditch will inevitably lead to further drainage of the lake and further erosion of its ecological and social values.

Protected area status: The site has never received legal status as a protected area, although it has long been protected by Afghan rulers. There appears to remain a vague historical sense of government ownership, control and protection, and game guards are currently stationed at the site. The guards are staff of the Ministry of Agriculture and Animal Husbandry and their 'office' consists of a small wall tent pitched near the reedbeds. The land tenure status around Kole Hashmat Khan is uncertain and many settlements are encroaching on the wetland area. Recommendations for the protection and management of the wetland were prepared in 1978 by FAO, but never implemented[69].

Human settlements: Encroachment of houses has occurred on the southeastern shores of the lake in areas where there were once only agricultural fields and a dozen farmhouses. Some ten years ago, local commanders seized the land and settled homeless people on it. Also lying between the lake and the Kabul-Gardez highway is a very large carpentry and wood bazaar. A community of *jogis* or gypsies lives in tents at the south end of the lake. There was no evidence of occupation by Kuchis, as occurred in the 1970s. As urban populations increase, the dry wetland areas are currently being viewed as a potential site for housing construction and development.

Wildlife: The game guards reported 200–300 ducks per day during spring 2002. While these numbers are significant, they are less than the 33 000 that were recorded over the course of two years during the 1960s[70]. Unfortunately, no consistent survey data exist with which to determine trends. Quail nets were observed on the south end of the reed-covered area in clear view of the game guards' tent. This suggests that the guards' duties are not well understood and/or that their authority is weak.

Photographs repeated from the same location at Kole Hashmat Khan in 1977 and 2002

Reed cutting: Phragmites reeds in the middle of the dry lakebed were being harvested for sale as roof thatch. Apparently, the government sold the rights to harvest the reeds for 700 million Afghanis, or approximately US$14 000. One of the stated reasons for harvesting the grass is to reduce fire hazard. Loss of *Phragmites* destroys nesting and summering habitat for birds and was noted by the game guards as a major environmental concern.

Urban development reaches the edge of the Kole Hashmat Khan wetland

Post-Conflict Environmental Assessment

> **Changes in land-use around Kabul and Kole Hashmat Khan wetland between 1986 and 2002**

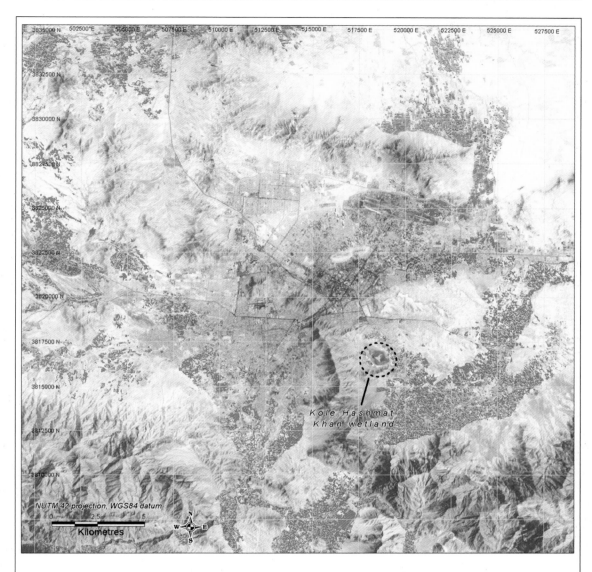

Kole Hashmat Khan wetland

NUTM 42 projection, WGS84 datum

Kilometres

Legend

- Change from cultivated to non-cultivated area
- Change from non-cultivated to cultivated area
- Satellite image backdrop (Landsat ETM+, 2002)

Note: the green polygons that appear on the Landsat image are unchanged cultivated areas

Changes in cultivated areas
Loss: 5 361 ha
Gain: 2 483 ha
———————
Total loss: 2 878 ha

About the map

Changes in cultivated areas cover derived from SPOT XS and Landsat ETM+ satellite imagery.

Date of image acquisitions:
1 July 1986 (XS)
27 July 2002 (ETM+)

Image processing: GEOIMAGE

UNEP

UNOSAT
satellite imagery for all

AFGHANISTAN

Dasht-e-Nawar National Waterfowl and Flamingo Sanctuary

Dasht-e-Nawar is an extensive high-altitude plain in southeast Afghanistan. Some 600 km² in area, the plain lies at about 3 350 m elevation, with surrounding peaks, holding ibex and urial, rising to 4 800 m. A narrow brackish lake, more than 10 km long, occurs in the plain. Dasht-e-Nawar serves as an important breeding and staging ground for a large number of migratory waterfowl. There are records of breeding populations of avocets (*Recurvirosta avocetta*), redshanks (*Tringa totanus*), greater sandplovers (*Charadrius leschenaultia),* and common terns (*Sterna hirundo*)[71]. The area is also a unique, high-elevation breeding ground for greater flamingo.

Key findings:

Hydrological condition: The lake proper was dry in 2002 and had disappeared in summer for the past four years. The recent drought appears to be the main cause of desiccation. However, there are small ponds and streams created by spring waters located near villages on the west side of the basin. Water for irrigation is nevertheless scarce and derived mostly from springs arising in the hillsides. Water is distributed under a traditional system of allocation. Crops and grazing for livestock were reported to be poor; flocks had declined greatly during the conflict, while the area devoted to dry land farming has increased. Local people reported that the major impact of the lake drying out was a decline in atmospheric humidity and a drying of soils leading to less abundant crops and poorer livestock grazing.

PETER ZAHLER/UNEP, 2002

UNEP driving across dry lakebed at Dasht-e-Nawar

Protected area status: This site was declared as a National Waterfowl and Flamingo Sanctuary in 1974, however its current legal status is unclear. The general consensus is that the protection previously afforded Dasht-e-Nawar is no longer in effect. The site has also previously been identified as meeting the criteria for listing as an internationally important site for migratory and breeding waterbirds under the Ramsar Convention. Recommendations for the protection and management of the site were prepared by FAO in 1977, but never implemented[72].

Human settlements: There are approximately 24 000 people living in a large number of villages distributed mostly on the west side of the wetland. The population is exclusively agro-pastoralist, producing wheat for subsistence and sheep, goats and cattle for milk, milk products and wool. Wool is utilized to weave *'gilim'* rugs and to knit gloves and sweaters. Prior to the drought, Dasht-e-Nawar was considered a 'bread-basket' region, supplying abundant food products to the Ghazni market. According to local people, the family average for goat and sheep herds has declined from pre-war levels of about 50 to near 0, and the number of cows has decreased from 10 to 1 or 2.

Post-Conflict Environmental Assessment

CHRIS SHANK/UNEP, 2002

Identifing waterfowl from the dry surface of the wetland

Wildlife: Although the lake was dry during the UNEP visit, small ponds and streams exist on the west side of the lake, created by natural spring waters. In these oases, UNEP observed several species of ducks, shorebirds, and waterbirds, including several grey heron (*Ardea cinerea*), pochard (*Aythya ferina*), mallard (*Anas platyrhynchos*), and large flocks of teal (*Anas* sp.). According to local reports, the mountains to the west of Dasht-e-Nawar area still support a small population of Himalayan ibex and urial. Local residents indicated that ungulates can sometimes be sighted in the nearby mountains during winter months. Some big game hunting is undertaken by local people, but it appears to be minimal, and almost no waterfowl hunting takes place. Locals are particularly averse to hunting flamingos because they associate the pink colour of the plumage with the blood of the martyred Imam Hussain. The villagers of Qarya said that they had seen one flamingo in 2002 and eight in 2001 but that no flamingos had successfully bred in the previous four years.

Ab-e-Estada National Waterfowl and Flamingo Sanctuary

Ab-e-Estada is a large saline lake located at about 2 000 m elevation in the southern foothills of the Hindu Kush. The site is remarkable for the large numbers of greater flamingos that breed on the islands. Flamingos arrive at high water levels in late March or April and depart when water levels decline in late September or early October. Numbers have varied, ranging from none in some years, up to 9 000 in others[73]. More than 100 other bird species also occur. The site was once a critical stopover point for the central population of Siberian cranes which bred in the Russian tundra and wintered in north-central India.

Key findings:

Hydrological condition: The lakebed and inflow rivers were completely dry during the UNEP visit. The combined Gardez, Ghazni, and Nahara Rivers were also dry as they entered Ab-e-Estada in the northeast. A well that had been hand-dug by Kuchis at the north end of the lake showed that the water table was approximately 3 m below surface level. According to local people, the lake has dried each year since 1999. In spring 2002 the lake filled for a brief period but was dry again within 10–15 days. Desiccation of the wetland is attributed to a combination of drought, damming of inflow rivers and water extraction by tube-wells

AFGHANISTAN

around the lake edge. Settlements have developed in recent years, and numbers of people are liable to increase as returning refugees move in. Local villagers are growing wheat and large quantities of water-intensive crops such as melons, almonds and grapes using irrigation from *karez* systems and, increasingly, water from deep wells. There are currently about 30 water pumps on the west side of the lake and as many as 150 in Nawa woleswali.

PETER ZAHLER/UNEP, 2002

UNEP team on dry surface of Ab-e-Estada

Protected area status: This site was declared a National Waterfowl and Flamingo Sanctuary in 1977, causing considerable resentment among local residents, many of whom are active waterfowl and flamingo hunters. Its current legal status is unclear. It had previously been identified as internationally important for migratory and breeding waterbirds and was recommended for inclusion on the list of internationally important wetlands at the first meeting of the Ramsar Convention in 1971. Recommendations for the protection and management of the site were prepared by FAO in 1977, but never implemented[74].

PETER ZAHLER/UNEP, 2002

10 cm cracks in dry Gardez riverbed at Ab-e-Estada

Human settlements: Historically there were no settlements in the semi-desert around Ab-e-Estada, although nomads from Kandahar visited the area in summer. In the recent past, Ghelzai Tarakai nomads settled at Ab-e-Estada and throughout Nawa[75]. Currently, there are eight villages lying within 10 km of Ab-e-Estada, with a total population of approximately 5 000[76]. Numbers are increasing rapidly with the return of displaced persons and with natural population increase. Local people are active waterfowl and flamingo hunters. There was considerable resentment over the protected status of the area during the 1970s. It is unlikely that local people would support renewed protection of Ab-e-Estada without extensive consultations and education programmes focused on raising awareness of environmental issues, especially community dependence and effects on the watershed.

PETER ZAHLER/UNEP, 2002

Local falcon hunter with kestrel as bait

Wildlife: Ab-e-Estada was once a critical stopover for the central population of Siberian cranes. In 1977, their numbers were estimated at only 57 individuals[77]. The International Crane Foundation states that of the central flyway population only two adults and one juvenile were recorded in 1997. The last reliable report of a Siberian crane at Ab-e-Estada was of one shot in 1986. Local residents reported that no flamingos had bred successfully for the past four years. Numerous falcon trappers were observed on the dry flats of Ab-e-Estada. Their main targets

PETER ZAHLER/UNEP, 2002

Abandoned flamingo nest at Ab-e-Estada

are saker *(Falco cherrug)* and peregrine falcons *(Falco peregrinus)*, which can reportedly be sold to local dealers for as much as 200 000 Pakistani rupees (US$3 400).

Imam Sahib Wildlife Managed Reserve

UNEP also visited *tugai* forest islands in the Amu Darya. Tugai is an important and characteristic wetland ecosystem type in the dry lands of central Asia, and along the Amu Darya is home to Eurasian otter *(Lutra lutra)*, wild boar and the endangered Bactrian deer *(Cervus elaphus bactrianus)*, as well as waterbirds and birds of prey. Because of the rarity of this ecosystem within Afghanistan, two island chains with tugai forest, Imam Sahib and Darqad, were proposed for protected area status in 1981[78]. UNEP attempted to visit both sites to assess current conditions but was only able to access the riverbank adjacent to the islands of Imam Sahib.

Key findings:

Protected area status: Both Imam Sahib and Darqad were declared as Royal Hunting Reserves in the last century, and restrictions were placed on settlements, hunting, cultivation and fuelwood collection. However, neither reserve was officially gazetted nor provided with a specific boundary description. FAO recommended in 1981 that both Imam Sahib and Darqad be considered for protected area status, but no action was ever taken[79]. Local people reported to UNEP that Imam Sahib was also designated as an official government reserve in the mid-1990s. However, government officials in the Ministry of Agriculture could not confirm this. Prior to the Taliban period and recent drought, government administrators noted that the reserve status was widely respected by local residents, and that prohibited land-use activities were generally not conducted.

Human settlements: In the last five years approximately 300 families settled on Imam Sahib in a bid to flee from Taliban rule. At the time of the UNEP visit it was reported that 200 families had since left the island. The remaining inhabitants are reported to be cutting the forests for fuelwood and clearing land for growing crops on the fertile soils.

Forest cover: The forested island chain of Imam Sahib was estimated by the local administrator to be 100 km long with widths varying from 1 to 10 km. From the riverbank, UNEP was able to observe intact forests of popular, willow and tamarisk. Local residents reported

MARTYN MURRAY/UNEP, 2002

Tugai forested islands of Imam Sahib

that while some forests have been cut by the new residents, the overall vegetation cover remains in good condition. Some local people were also familiar with Darqad and estimated that the forested island chain stretches for about 50 km in length and up to 5 km in width. However, the ecological and protected status of the island were unknown.

Wildlife: Local administrators reported that Imam Sahib contains populations of wild boar, fox, hare, Bactrian deer, porcupine, eagle, falcon and pheasant. However, UNEP could not confirm this report, nor collect any supporting evidence such as tracks, dung, feathers or fur.

Ajar Valley Wildlife Reserve

The Ajar Valley is comprised of east-west trending ridges with peaks rising to an elevation of 3,800 m. The spectacularly sheer-sided Jawzari Canyon (Dara-e-Jawzari) was cut by the Ajar River and bisects the area from east to west. The river now runs underground for most of the length of Jawzari and flows directly from the canyon wall at the spring of Chiltan. Downstream, a natural dam has created picturesque Lake Chiltan. The rulers of Afghanistan have long used the Ajar Valley as a hunting area. Amir Habibullah built a lodge in Dara-e-Jawzari in the early 1900s and constructed the current trail into the valley. King Zahir Shah bought about 200 ha of land at the mouth of Dara-e-Jawzari in the 1950s and built a hunting lodge near the Ajar River.

During the mid-1970s, FAO estimated ibex numbers at approximately 2 350 based on actual survey results, but accepted an estimate of 5 000 made by a local hunter as being feasible[80]. Urial were found to be much rarer, but no population estimates were provided. Bactrian deer were introduced in 1955 from the Darqad wetlands on the Amu Darya River and were reported to number 26 animals in 1976. As a consequence of relatively undisturbed habitat, birds were reported by FAO as more diverse than elsewhere in the central Hindu Kush. Snow leopard, common leopard *(Panthera pardus)*, lynx *(Lynx lynx)*, wolf, red fox, Eurasian otter, and stone marten *(Martes foina)* were all found in the reserve area, although no population estimates were available.

UNEP attempted to visit the Ajar valley to determine the current ecological and institutional status of the protected area. However, due to ongoing conflict in the area, access was not permitted. The last assessment of the valley was conducted by an indigenous Afghan NGO, Save the Environment Afghanistan (SEA), in 1999 with funding from WWF-Pakistan[81]. The following preliminary findings are taken from this study, as well as from interviews with government officials and other background materials.

Key Findings:

Protected area status: The Ajar Valley was gazetted as a Wildlife Sanctuary in June 1977 and a preliminary management plan was developed by FAO in the same year[82]. However, there appear to be no official records documenting the exact boundaries of the reserve. Estimates of the likely boundaries conclude that the reserve comprised approximately 50 000 ha[83].

Human settlements: The land tenure in the Ajar Valley is reported to be uncertain. It appears that local commanders effectively own the land as a fiefdom. The area is reportedly being cultivated and grazed on a share-cropping basis by a recent influx of colonizers. It is reported that local people are unaware of the area's special status and importance[84].

Wildlife: Information obtained from sources was not consistent or complete, but the general pattern is clear and can be summarized as follows[85]. Hunting occurs throughout the area. At present ibex are much reduced in number, and only a few hundred may remain. Urial have fared more poorly than ibex and only a very few survive. Bactrian deer and feral yaks no longer exist. Wolves remain, but common leopard and snow leopard may be gone. The juniper trees and willows are largely gone, and deforestation is continuing. Fishing pressure in Lake Chiltan and the Ajar River is intense through the use of electrocution, grenades, and rockets.

Hamoun-i-Puzak Waterfowl Sanctuary

The wetland of Hamoun-i-Puzak is located in southwestern Afghanistan in the Sistan depression of the Helmand Basin. In 1971, Hamoun-i-Puzak was one of the most important wetlands in Afghanistan for

CHRIS SHANK/FAO,1976

Ajar valley in 1976

migrating waterfowl. Up to half-a-million waterfowl were counted in the 1970s[86], representing roughly 150 species of migrating and non-migrating birds[87]. The area is often reported to be an official waterfowl sanctuary, but it has never been gazetted. As a result, it currently has no protection status. It was recommended for designation as a national park by FAO in 1981, but no action was taken[88].

UNEP visited this site during its assessment of the Helmand River basin. A more detailed site description and findings, including satellite-image analyses, are given on page 50.

Pamir-e-Buzurg Wildlife Reserve

The Pamir-e-Buzurg Wildlife Reserve is located in the western 'panhandle' of land known as the Wakhan Corridor. The area was originally established by King Zahir Shah as a royal hunting reserve. It was formally established and gazetted in 1978 in an effort to protect its unique wildlife, in particular the famous Marco Polo wild sheep. The area is also home to other mountain ungulates such as Siberian ibex (*Capra ibex sibericus*) and large predator species such the snow leopard and brown bear.

UNEP visited this site during its assessment of the Wakhan Corridor. A more detailed site description and findings follow.

■ The Wakhan Corridor

The Wakhan Corridor is a narrow strip of alpine valleys and high mountains that stretches eastward from the province of Badakhshan following the headwaters of the Amu Darya River to its source in the Pamir Mountains. It borders with Tajikistan to the north, Pakistan to the south and China to the east. It is more than 200 km long (east to west) and between

Ibex and Marco Polo sheep horns mark the grave of a saint in the Wakhan Corridor

Wakhi family milking yaks

20 and 60 km broad (north to south), covering a total area of about 10 300 km². This includes the easternmost ranges of the Hindu Kush and the south-easternmost part of the greater Pamir range to a point where they join the Karakorams.

The Wakhan is divided into three geographical sections: the main Wakhan strip between Ishkeshem and Qala Panja and the Pamir knot, which is made up of two blocks of high mountains, the Pamir-e-Kalan or Pamir-i-Buzurg (Big Pamir), and the Pamir-e-Khord (Little Pamir). Big Pamir was once declared a royal hunting reserve and was designated a wildlife reserve in 1978. The name Big Pamir refers to the mountain range rising to some 6 900 m in the middle section of the Wakhan.

The Wakhan is of unique interest both from the point of view of its environment and biodiversity and from its human population. The complex terrain has long provided a route for traders and Kyrgyz herders who, like the rare and endangered Marco Polo sheep move from place to place according to season and the availability of grazing. The yurt-dwelling Kyrgyz live both in the Big Pamir and Little Pamir, at the eastern end of the corridor. The grazing lands are also used by resident Wakhi farmers and herders, who are based mainly along the Wakhan valley west of Pamir-i-Buzurg and keep camels and yaks, as well as sheep, goats and cattle. The Wakhi are followers of the Aga Khan, adhering to the Ismaili branch of the Muslim faith.

The object of UNEP's visit to the Wakhan Corridor was to collect information on the overall state of the environment in the Wakhan, as well as investigate key social, economic and institutional pressures. In particular, UNEP focused on assessing the current status of the Pamir-i-Buzurg Wildlife Reserve. Due to the remoteness of the area it is rarely visited by UN missions, and UNEP entered the region on horseback for a period of two weeks from 20 September to 10 October 2002.

AFGHANISTAN

NATURAL RESOURCES

87

4

Snow leopard. Insert: snow leopard tracks in the Warwarm valley region

UNEP

CHARUDUTT MISHRA/UNEP, 2002

Key findings:

Wildlife: UNEP confirmed that snow leopards apparently occur throughout the Wakhan region, including the Pamir-i-Buzurg reserve area and between Ishkeshem and Qala-e-Oanja in the corridor west of this area, principally in the mountains along its southern fringe.

UNEP also made visual sightings of two herds of Marco Polo sheep in the Shikargah Valley of the Big Pamir. Local reports indicated this species is now restricted to the Pamir-i-Buzurg Wildlife Reserve and the Little Pamir, with higher numbers in the latter area. UNEP collected direct or verbal evidence of wolf, brown bear, Asian ibex and urial, red fox, cape hare *(Lepus capensis)*, stone marten and long-tailed marmots *(Marmota caudata)*. UNEP was unable to locate any fresh signs of lynx during the survey. A total of 50 bird species were also sighted while en route, of which ten species are new additions to the list of 117 species previously compiled in 1978[89].

ANTHONY FITZHERBERT/UNEP, 2002

UNEP

Brown bear. Insert: brown bear scat in the Yupgaz valley region

Post-Conflict Environmental Assessment

CHRIS SHANK/UNEP, 2002

Snow leopard skin in Chicken Street fur shop, Kabul

Livestock predation: UNEP observed that the age-old conflict between herders and snow leopard (as well as wolf and bear) continues to be a key problem. Interview results suggested important differences between snow leopards and wolves in the patterns of livestock predation. Wolves were reported to take livestock throughout the year, while most cases of snow leopard killing livestock were reported in winter. All wolf kills were reported from pastures or from near settlements where livestock were penned out in the open. Most snow leopard attacks, on the other hand, involved instances of the animal entering a corral. Consequently, unlike the wolves, the snow leopard attacks were reported to result frequently in excessive surplus killing of livestock. For this reason, snow leopards face the brunt of people's retaliation against livestock predation in the Wakhan. Numerous cases were reported of snow leopards being shot.

Hunting: Reportedly, hunting pressure on wildlife was much reduced during the Soviet occupation, but has increased subsequently. UNEP noted that the Wakhi have responded positively to the call made by the Afghan Transitional Authority to hand in arms and stop hunting. At present, the trade in wildlife furs at the local level in the Wakhan Corridor is at best casual, and most of the hunting is for meat. This was further confirmed by the total absence of any wildlife trade in the Ishkeshem and Faizabad markets. Snow leopards are killed mostly in retaliation against livestock predation. When such instances take place, the skin is preserved and sold to passing traders. The situation is, however, different in other regions of Badakhshan province, where active hunting of endangered snow leopards is taking place. UNEP observed that snow leopard skins from Badakshan are being sold in fur markets in Kabul, primarily to western aid workers and soldiers. While these buyers may be unaware of its endangered status, their actions may encourage poachers to increase the snow leopard hunt, driving the species closer to extinction in Afghanistan.

Livestock grazing: Grazing land was in reasonable condition at lower elevations, but appeared to be increasingly degraded in the Ishtemich/Shikargah valley region at heights between

4 000 and 4 400 m, above which lie the alpine meadows grazed by Marco Polo sheep in summer. A trend toward keeping stock in this zone year-round appears to be developing, raising concerns that this may deny grazing to Marco Polo sheep due to disturbance or competition.

High-elevation grazing in the Yupgaz region

Climate change: Oral testimony provided by a Kyrgyz leader in the 1970s, before current concerns over the magnitude and impact of global climate change emerged, indicated that significant changes were then taking place in the climate of the Wakhan. Autumn rains and winter snow used to be regular, but over the decades leading to the 1970s both had diminished greatly in quantity, and glaciers had retreated to the highest valleys. Traditional grazing lands became less productive, forcing pastoralists to seek grazing at higher elevations. Although it is difficult to quantify such reported changes, it is clear that continuing climate change has the potential to severely affect livelihoods in the region.

Food security: Food security is a continuing difficulty, with shortages common in spring and early summer when food stocks are depleted prior to the next harvest. The situation has been alleviated to some extent by work undertaken by the NGO Focus, an Aga Khan-supported development organization. Reducing the chronic addiction to opium that is prevalent in the Wakhan is likely to be a more difficult problem.

Wheat harvest in Qazi Deh region

Post-Conflict Environmental Assessment

Shikargah valley region where Marco Polo rams were spotted

Landmines: The Wakhan Corridor was mostly spared the turmoil of military conflict, and mines were not laid, avoiding the major problem they present elsewhere in the country.

Protected area status: The Pamir-i-Buzurg Wildlife Reserve was officially gazetted in 1978. However, the current status of protection afforded to the reserve is unclear given recent institutional changes. The wildlife reserve is situated in an isolated area with low human population densities, thus offering good conditions for wildlife protection. However, given the mobility of human and wildlife populations and the traditional trading links through the Wakhan, consideration should be given to expanding the area of protected lands. An opportunity exists to link management activities with other protected areas in the region. Over time, the Wakhan Corridor could become an important component of a transboundary protected area, linked to other existing or proposed sites in China, Pakistan and Tajikistan.

UNEP/FAO expert on horseback in the Wakhan Corridor

5 Environmental governance

Prior to the foreign occupation of 1979, the government of Afghanistan was already taking modest steps to address some of the environmental problems of the country, especially those of water supply, deforestation and wildlife conservation. As early as 1972, the government requested assistance from UNDP and FAO in developing a strategy for the conservation and management of natural resources and wildlife. The strategy was eventually published in 1981[90]. It provided detailed information on the physical and biological environment of Afghanistan, as well as its ecological history and current conservation challenges in the areas of forestry, agriculture, endangered species, wetland management, legislation, and education.

To identify the most pressing institutional, policy and legal needs for environmental management, UNEP collected information on the current organization of the environmental sector. The following sections provide a broad overview of existing government structures, policies, laws and instruments for environmental management. Recommendations for building the necessary institutional capacity are given in Chapter 6.

Institutional framework

The historical transition to a new government in Afghanistan took place in December 2001 with the signing of the Bonn Agreement ('Agreement on Provisional Arrangements in Afghanistan Pending the Re-establishment of Permanent Government Institutions'). The agreement established the Afghan Interim Administration (AIA), consisting of a Chairman, Mr Hamid Karzai, five Vice-Chairmen and 24 other members. A Supreme Court of Afghanistan was also established.

One of the primary tasks of the new administration was to prepare for an emergency *loya jirga* (or 'grand assembly') within six months. It convened in June 2002 and was opened by the former King of Afghanistan, Zahir Shah. The *loya jirga* decided on the composition of a broad-based Transitional Authority, led by Hamid Karzai and a cabinet of 31 ministers. The Transitional Authority will lead Afghanistan until a fully representative government can be elected within two years.

■ Ministry of Irrigation, Water Resources and Environment

For the first time in the history of the country, an authority for environmental management was mandated in the new governmental structure. The Ministry of Irrigation and Water Resources (established under the Interim Administration) was allocated the additional responsibility for environmental management and renamed as the Ministry of Irrigation, Water Resources and Environment (MIWRE).

The mandate of the new ministry covers watershed management, including the maintenance, design and construction of water intakes, irrigation canals, and reservoirs as well as the ecological condition of catchments. Responsibility for environmental management as well as environmental degradation was also added to its mandate.

When MIWRE was established, the country's environmental priorities had not been elaborated or prioritized, and the ministry operated largely without any policy guidance. Its current vision for environmental management reflects a traditional, sectoral approach, consisting of 700 staff members and individual units covering sanitation, hazardous waste, industry, agriculture, pollution, emergencies and disasters, and international relations. The operational plan divides the country into the five major water basins, with the Department of Irrigation representing MIWRE at the provincial and district levels.

The ministry has one minister, two deputy ministers (one technical, one administrative), and twelve directorates general. The technical deputy minister is responsible for the planning and implementation of irrigation and water resources programmes. The administrative deputy minister is responsible for the operational side of management, such as contracts, staffing and maintenance of buildings. The twelve directorates general are organized along functional responsibilities including education, technical, construction, design, engineering, planning, administration, liaison, forestry, and irrigation.

A Department of Environment has been created, but it does not at present have dedicated staff to work specifically on environmental management issues. Rather, the staff consists mainly of technical water and irrigation experts, consultants and engineers. Currently, the core environmental staff in the Department of Environment is composed of only the minister, the deputy minister responsible for environmental affairs and the director of planning. Capacity building and technical assistance is currently being provided to the ministry by UNEP, as well as other UN agencies including UNESCO and UNICEF.

■ Other relevant environmental management bodies

In addition to MIWRE, a number of other sector ministries and bodies also have significant environmental responsibilities:

- **Afghan Assistance Coordination Authority (AACA):** The AACA was created as a temporary institution to review and approve all reconstruction projects conducted by international agencies and bilateral donors. It also facilitates the management, coordination and financial tracking of reconstruction efforts, and is responsible for government-wide capacity building strategies. AACA is governed by a board consisting of Hamid Karzai, the Ministers of Finance, Planning, and Reconstruction, the head of the Central Bank, the Director of AACA and several eminent individuals from the private and non-governmental sectors. AACA has led the coordination of the National Development Framework and Budget.

- **Ministry of Finance:** This ministry's main responsibility is to prepare and monitor, in cooperation with other ministries, the state budget. This involves determining financial and monetary policies and channeling financial contributions through the appropriate funding mechanisms.

- **Ministry of Reconstruction:** The ministry is responsible for overall policy development on reconstruction priorities and for coordinating international assistance.

- **Ministry of Planning:** This ministry is responsible for planning coordination and ensuring harmony with national policies and reconstruction priorities. Annual plans developed by each ministry will be forwarded to the Ministry of Planning for review and consolidation. They will then be incorporated into the national budget deliberations of the Ministry of Finance.

- **Ministry of Agriculture and Animal Husbandry:** This ministry has traditionally held and continues to hold responsibility for the management of key environmental sectors including forests, wildlife, wetlands and fisheries. It is also responsible for agricultural and rangelands, including cultivation, grazing and chemicals management. Protected areas management was conducted in cooperation with the Afghanistan Tourist Organization. This ministry is a critical partner to the Ministry of Irrigation, Water Resources and Environment in field-level implementation of environmental policy and enforcement of regulations. Capacity building and technical assistance to the ministry is currently being provided by the FAO. Prior to the period of conflict, the ministry was represented in all provinces and in multiple districts. Many of these offices are staffed but are not conducting management activities due to a lack of capacity and equipment.

- **Ministry of Public Health:** This ministry is divided into a preventative section and a treatment section. A Department of Environmental Health was first established in 1976. This department addresses health issues related to environmental pollution, such as air pollution-related diseases (respiratory infections, dust and smog), water pollution and sanitation-related diseases (intestinal, cholera, diarrhea) and liquid and solid waste-related diseases (infections, flies, rats, mosquitoes). In principle, the Department of Environmental Health has an environmental monitoring responsibility. However, it is currently unable to perform this function since laboratory facilities have been largely destroyed. The ministry is also responsible for the clean-up of environmental contamination, food safety of both imported and manufactured foods, and provision of environmental inspectors to cities. WHO is assisting the Ministry of Public Health with a variety of health-related activities.

- **Ministry of Urban Development and Housing:** The ministry is responsible for the construction of housing, city planning, water supply and sewage systems and has established an environmental department. In principle, the ministry works closely with the municipalities. UN-Habitat supports many of their programmes, including those on urban waste, water, and sanitation.

- **Ministry of Rural Rehabilitation and Development:** Overall responsibility for rural livelihoods rests with this ministry. This includes a variety of activities from provision of seeds and medicines, to the construction of clinics, schools and village roads, to the management of village water supplies. The mandate of this ministry clearly overlaps with many other ministries. Due to the broad mandate of this ministry, which clearly overlaps with many other ministries, it works closely with a variety of UN agencies, in particular the UNDP Area Based Development Programme.

- **Ministry of Water and Power:** This ministry has responsibility for national power supply, planning and reconstruction of hydropower dams, and management of surface water and reservoirs. It does not have an environmental department and limited collaboration is conducted with other ministries with water management mandates.

- **Ministry of Mines and Industry:** Responsibilities for the development and management of mines and heavy industry, including wastes, are allocated to this ministry. At present it has neither an environmental department, nor the capacity for considering environmental impacts of mining or industrial production.

- **Ministry of Information and Culture:** This ministry is responsible for the collection and distribution of information and for media. Responsibility for the organization of environmental information has not been clarified. At an operational level, the ministry has responsibility for the management of national heritage sites, museums, and cultural centres.

- **Ministry of Foreign Affairs:** Responsibilities for international and regional environmental cooperation lie with this ministry, including participation in international environmental conventions.

■ Local governance

Afghanistan has always been rich in cultural diversity and regional differences. Throughout its national history, governance has been largely based on the provincial, municipal and local levels, rather than centrally led from Kabul. An important traditional decision-making body at the village level is known as a *shura* (in Dari) or *jirga* (in Pashto). Typically, the village mullah and male elders would select a village *Arbab* (in Dari) or *Malik* (in Pashto) to make key community decisions, represent the community at the provincial or national level and resolve disputes between community members and neighbouring villages.

Natural resources were also often managed at the community level. For example, water resources were frequently managed by a *Mirab* (water master) elected by farmers to make key decisions on water distribution, operations and maintenance, as well as to be the link to government water authority personnel. In many regions, woodlands and rangelands were monitored by community-based wardens or rangers. Penalties for illegal wood cutting included fines per kg of wood cut and up to three months in jail. Fines of up to US$8 were also imposed for illegal cultivation of woodlands and pasture lands. Cutting forests for commercial purposes resulted in jail terms of 1 to 10 years. Prior to the development of a national legal framework, local traditions and customs formed the law of each village. Urban centres also developed their own municipal laws and standards and found solutions to the problems of waste management, water supply, transportation, and energy.

With the onset of conflict, many local decision-making systems collapsed, leaving an institutional void across the country. In some areas, local commanders took power and imposed their own systems of governance. In others, local communities maintained a high level of autonomy and decision-making authority, and strongly resisted all instances of external interference. One general trend was that local community decision-making structures became unable to deal with the magnitude of the demands being made on the environment, as well as the resulting environmental degradation. Across the country, responsibilities for resource management and urban environmental needs could only be partially met due to a lack of information, damaged land base and infrastructure, and a lack of financial resources and human capacity.

Given that nearly 80 per cent of the population is located in rural areas, the government has identified a strong future role for local-level and community-based environmental management. Presently, some regions are still heavily influenced by commanders with policies that contradict those of the central government. In other regions, the rule of law is being enforced and central government is gaining influence and control. Attempts are being made by the Transitional Authority to ensure municipal revenues, taxes and customs fees flow to the central government. Governors that display vested interests in the local economy are being replaced and budget allocations from central government to the local level are contingent on the enforcement of the rule of law.

Legislative framework

In the current transitional period, the Bonn Agreement determined that the 1964 constitution enacted under the monarchy shall continue to govern Afghanistan's legal system, to the extent that it is not inconsistent with other components of the Agreement. Laws adopted between 1964 and 1973 are applicable on an interim basis to the extent that their provisions are not inconsistent with the Bonn Agreement. Laws enacted after 1973 are also valid provided they do not conflict with the Bonn Agreement, or laws enacted between 1964 and 1973. The Transitional Authority has power and authority to repeal or amend such laws as it sees fit.

5

A Constitutional Commission (Drafting Committee) and a Secretary for the Constitutional Commission have been appointed by the Transitional Authority in accordance with the provisions of the Bonn Agreement. The new constitution will be reviewed at a special *loya jirga*, to be convened before December 2003.

In November 2002 a commission to rebuild the judicial sector was also established, consisting of nine officials representing different ethnic groups in Afghanistan. The commission, also a requirement of the Bonn Agreement, will begin rebuilding the domestic justice system in accordance with Islamic principles, international standards, the rule of law and Afghan legal traditions.

■ Environmental laws

Based on this legal framework, the Department of Law, Ministry of Justice has identified the following laws as containing important and valid environmental provisions:

Water Law	**1981**
The Forestry Law of Islamic Emirate of Afghanistan	**2000**
The Islamic Emirate of Afghanistan Law for Land Ownership	**2000**
Nature Protection Law	**1986 / 2000**
Agricultural Quarantine Services Law	**2000**
Veterinary Services Law	**2000**
Hunting and Wildlife Protection Law	**2000**
Range Management Law	**1970 / 2000**
Agriculture Cooperative Development Law	**2000**
Charter for Department of Fertilizer and Agro-Chemicals	**2000**
Seed Improvement Department Charter	**2000**

However, none of the current laws accurately reflect the new institutional arrangements, or contain modern provisions for environmental management.

The Department of Environment of MIWRE has begun the process of drafting a new environmental framework law. The development process is taking place before the existence of government environmental policy and clarification of ministry mandates. This approach is contrary to standard procedures, whereby framework laws are developed after policies have been formulated and mandates defined. As a result, if future policies are contrary to the law, revisions may be necessary to ensure harmony.

With new environmental policies yet to be defined, no new environmental legislation has been developed by any of the line ministries. The Transitional Authority is, however, adamant that the country needs strict and enforceable environmental laws if it is to achieve sustainable use and rehabilitation of the resource base. Some priority sectors have already

Post-Conflict Environmental Assessment

been identified including water, forests and endangered species. It is envisioned that each of the sector ministries will be responsible for drafting sectoral environmental laws. Each draft law will be reviewed by the Ministry of Justice and amended according to the prevailing justice policies, jurisprudence and common practices. A development, review or coordination role for the Ministry of Irrigation, Water Resources and Environment has not yet been defined. Moreover, little consideration has been given to developing a process for public review.

In the absence of new environmental laws, the Transitional Authority has issued various decrees banning hunting and timber harvesting in order to protect the declining resource base. However, the decrees are difficult to enforce and do not cover all environmental management issues.

■ Monitoring and enforcement

Due to the lack of human resources, equipment, funding and capacity, there is little or no active monitoring or enforcement of existing laws or new decrees. UNEP found that the recent decrees were effective in some areas and totally ineffective in others. For example, residents of the Wakhan Corridor were very aware and respectful of the ban on hunting. On the other hand, the logging ban is largely being ignored in the eastern provinces due to disputes over resource ownership, as well as commander influence. The Ministry of Agriculture and Animal Husbandry has proposed to assign 300 forest protection guards to Kunar Province (also called 'green forces') to enforce the ban.

■ Environmental Impact Assessment

Environmental Impact Assessment (EIA) is a planning tool to promote sustainable development by integrating environmental costs and benefits into proposed development activities. In the long term, it should minimize environmental impacts and save costs by preventing unnecessary environmental degradation. Limited forms of EIA can be used to ensure smaller-scale projects conform to appropriate environmental standards and design criteria.

A process for conducting EIA of all humanitarian and reconstruction projects is absent from Afghanistan's legal framework. As a result many projects, such as deep-well drilling or large-scale irrigation schemes, are being conducted without considering regional or long-term impacts and environmental costs. There is also no consistent application of EIA guidelines used by donors and international organizations.

The Transitional Authority has expressed a strong interest in mainstreaming an EIA process for future reconstruction and development projects. Some discussions have taken place between key ministries on establishing an inter-ministerial EIA task force, but no final decisions have been made.

Policy framework

One of the first tasks of the Afghan Interim Administration was to draft a National Development Framework (NDF) – a basic document outlining the administration's strategy for reconstruction and development.

The first draft, released in April 2002, outlined that the private sector would become the major engine of economic growth for the country. International assistance would be sought to rebuild the basic infrastructures and institutions needed to allow private investment and human capital to flourish. Cross-cutting issues identified were security, administrative and financial reform, and gender.

The NDF identified twelve programmes as priorities for national development. All international assistance was required to be consistent with the development priorities outlined in the document – a way to ensure Afghan ownership of the reconstruction process.

In order to elaborate each of the 12 priority programmes, programme groups were established consisting of relevant ministries and UN partners. The groups attempted to translate the priorities of the NDF into a National Development Budget (NDB), while simultaneously providing a vehicle for policy development. The NDB, covering the Afghan lunar year 1381–1382, was released on 10 October 2002. The estimated budget needs totalled nearly US$3.2 billion dollars.

■ Environmental policy development

One of the programme groups established by the NDF focused on natural resource management. Membership consisted of the Ministry of Agriculture and Animal Husbandry, the Ministry of Rural Rehabilitation and Development and the Ministry of Irrigation, Water Resources and Environment. UN partners included FAO and UNEP.

The group was mandated to develop sub-programmes to improve livelihoods through sustainable resource management and rehabilitation. The strong need for environmental protection and management was identified as an important area for national development. The following seven sub-programmes were eventually identified requiring a budget amounting to US$171 million:

1	Institutional Strengthening
2	Rehabilitation and Sustainable Development of Agriculture
3	Horticulture Rehabilitation and Development
4	Livestock Rehabilitation and Development
5	Water Resources, Forest and Rangeland Management
6	Socio-economic Development for Rural and Peri-urban Populations
7	Environment Preservation and Regeneration

The ability of the government to implement projects in each of these sub-programmes will depend almost entirely on financial support from the international community. In addition, it will be essential to understand the linkages between each programme and to develop goals, targets and timetables within an overall framework document such as a National Environmental Action Plan (NEAP).

■ Environmental information

Due to the lack of modern framework and sectoral environmental laws, there is no systematic gathering of environmental data for monitoring conditions and influencing policy development. While some ministries reportedly undertake a limited amount of *ad hoc* data collection, it is not consistently collected or routinely shared. The lack of communications between the provinces and central government also hampers data exchange. None of the ministries currently have adequate staff resources to collect environmental information, and in many cases monitoring facilities and equipment have been destroyed during the years of war.

Post-Conflict Environmental Assessment

International framework

Transforming Afghanistan into a prosperous, democratic and self-sustaining country cannot be achieved without the assistance of the international community. The Afghan Reconstruction Steering Group (ARSG), consisting of over 60 countries, the EU, G8 members, and UN/World Bank, was created to mobilize international funds for reconstruction efforts in Afghanistan.

UNDP, the World Bank and the Asian Development Bank conducted a preliminary needs assessment[91] of investment, technical assistance and institutional building costs for 19 sectors. The assessment estimated US$9–12 billion would be needed over a period of five years to address Afghanistan's immediate reconstruction needs. Approximately US$1.7 billion would be required in 2002.

The first major pledging conference was held on 21–22 January 2002 in Tokyo. The AIA presented its vision for Afghanistan's development and reconstruction. The international donor community responded by pledging over US$1.8 billion for the year 2002. Cumulative commitments, including multi-year pledges, equalled more than US$4.5 billion.

Following the Tokyo meeting, the UN formally launched the Immediate and Transitional Assistance Programme for Afghanistan (ITAP) in February[92]. The programme document outlines a comprehensive strategy, for which the financial requirements for 2002 totalled US$1.33 billion.

In order to establish short-, medium- and long-term priorities, the Afghan Assistance Coordination Authority (AACA) engaged in a consultation process with the relevant ministries and UN agencies to discuss the projects that were submitted for funding under ITAP. This consultation process resulted in an agreed list of AACA-approved projects totalling US$898 million for 2002.

In October 2002 the Transitional Authority and the UN agencies proceeded to prepare the 2003 Transitional Assistance Programme for Afghanistan (TAPA)[93] to reflect the funding needs identified in the National Development Budget. The TAPA outlines the UN programmes and projects for 2003/2004 which will respond to the continuing humanitarian crisis in Afghanistan, accelerate recovery and reconstruction initiatives started in 2002, and support regeneration of the capacity and institutions of local and central government.

■ International environmental assistance

The preliminary needs assessment noted that the serious degradation of the environment is a strong concern and that arresting and reversing environmental degradation should be a guiding principle during reconstruction. Environmental management and protection were not listed as a distinct sector, but were integrated into other sectors including Health, Water and Sanitation, Energy, Urban Development, Agriculture, and Natural Resource Management. The combined one-year cost estimates for these sectors were US$230 million. Specific figures for environmental investments in each of the sectors were not given.

The ITAP also integrated costs for environmental investments within other sectors. However, a sector entitled 'Food Security, Agriculture and Environment' was also established, entailing projects costing US$60 million in 2002.

The Asian Development Bank (ADB) indicated a strong commitment to the environment sector at the Tokyo pledging conference. Based on the decisions and share of responsibilities between World Bank, ADB and Islamic Development Bank, the ADB took the initiative and organized the preliminary needs assessment on environment. UNEP participated in this ADB-led mission to Kabul in March 2002. Among its assistance package to Afghanistan, the ADB has started to prepare a programme that aims to build up the minimum institutional capacities for natural resource management. ADB will also support the reconstruction of the energy and health sectors.

Environmental assistance provided by the suite of United Nations bodies was divided according to the comparative advantage of each agency. FAO focused on the rehabilitation of the agriculture, irrigation and livestock sectors. UNICEF was active in promoting a sustainable water resources management strategy and in rebuilding rural drinking water supplies and sanitation. UNESCO assessed needs for transboundary water cooperation and also addressed the cross-cutting issues of media development, education and the protection of cultural heritage sites. UN Habitat's programme targeted urban developments such as rehabilitation of housing, urban water supply, sanitation, and neighbourhood development. UNEP conducted a post-conflict environmental assessment to understand current conditions, threats and pressures on the environment, in order to identify the most urgent environmental priorities and needs.

In the latest donor appeal (TAPA), natural resources management is one of the 12 priority sectors. The estimated needs for the seven sub-programmes covering capacity building, rehabilitation, sustainable management, training and education in 2003/2004 total US$42 million. Labour intensive programmes for environmental restoration are being prioritized by the Transitional Authority. For example, an "Afghan Conservation Corps" has been proposed that will put thousands of former combatants back to work reforesting 18 locations across the country.

International and regional cooperation

■ Multilateral environmental agreements

Afghanistan has ratified and is currently a party to five major international environmental agreements. The first agreement, the Convention Concerning the Protection of World Cultural and Natural Heritage, was ratified in 1979[94]. The first and so far only Afghan site inscribed on the UNESCO World Heritage List is the minaret and associated archaeological remains at Jam, in Shahrak district, Ghowr province. The case for inclusion was reviewed by the World Heritage Commission and the site was listed in 2002. At the same time it was placed on the register of World Heritage sites in danger, largely because of recent damage and apparent attempts to steal archaeological objects. While potential World Heritage natural sites exist in Afghanistan, such as Pamir-i-Buzurg Wildlife Reserve and Band-e-Amir National Park, none have been officially listed by the convention.

In 1985 Afghanistan became a party to the Convention on International Trade in Endangered Species of Wild Fauna and Flora (CITES)[95]. The Convention to Combat Desertification (CCD) was ratified in 1995[96]. The Convention on Biological Diversity (CBD) and the United Nations Framework Convention on Climate Change (UNFCCC) were signed in 1992, but no immediate steps were taken towards ratification. These conventions were finally ratified in September 2002 by the Transitional Authority[97][98]. In 1989 the government signed but failed to ratify the Convention on the Control of Transboundary Movements of Hazardous Wastes and their Disposal[99] (commonly referred to as the Basel Convention).

Each convention that Afghanistan has ratified, or will ratify, will enable it to access technical support in terms of funds, training and other capacity-building activities. On the other hand, the country will also need to ensure it fulfils its obligations under each convention, enforcing their respective provisions at the national level.

■ Clean Development Mechanism, Kyoto Protocol

The National Development Framework identified a strong interest in benefiting from the Climate Change Convention's Kyoto Protocol. Under the protocol, ratifying nations agree to reduce their emissions of six different greenhouse gases to an average of 5.2 per cent below 1990 levels during the five-year period 2008 to 2012. For the protocol to take effect, 55 governments, including developed countries representing at least 55 per cent of that group's 1990 greenhouse gas emissions, must ratify the treaty. As of early October 2002, 95 parties had ratified, including developed countries responsible for 37.1 per cent of emissions.

As a means of achieving the goals of the protocol, three flexible mechanisms have been established for giving parties credit for reducing emissions in other countries. In other words, countries that find it expensive to reduce emissions at home can pay for cheaper emissions cuts elsewhere. The global economic efficiency of reducing emissions is increased while the overall 5 per cent reduction target is still met.

The first mechanism, known as 'emissions trading', allows countries that limit or reduce emissions more than is required by their agreed target to sell the excess emissions credits to countries that find it more difficult or more expensive to meet their own targets. The 'joint implementation' (JI) mechanism allows industrialized countries to obtain 'emissions reduction units' by financing projects in other developed countries that lead to emission reductions. Finally, the 'clean development mechanism' (CDM) will provide credit to industrialized countries for financing emission-reducing or emission-avoiding projects in developing countries.

The Afghan Transitional Authority has requested international assistance in developing the necessary institutional structures to benefit from the CDM. Although information was limited, UNEP attempted to calculate present and future carbon dioxide (CO_2) emissions and mitigation potentials in the energy, fuel and forestry sectors to enable opportunities to be identified.

According to planning figures from the Ministry of Water and Power, nearly 95 per cent of future electrical production will come from hydroelectric production. The remaining 5 per cent will come from natural gas, coal and crude oil power production. While hydro-production contributes zero emissions, the burning of fossil fuels was estimated to produce 1.6 million tonnes of CO_2 per year.

In urban centres, meeting transportation, cooking and lighting needs for 2003 is expected to be met largely through the use of petroleum products such as gasoline, kerosene and diesel fuel. The Ministry of Trade and Commerce estimates that 850 000 tonnes will be needed on a yearly basis in the immediate future. The resulting CO_2 emissions from this use would be nearly 2.7 million tonnes of CO_2 per year.

Compared to these figures, by far the greatest potential release of CO_2 may come from the burning of fuelwood. Based on an estimate of 18 million people depending exclusively on the use of fuelwood for heating and cooking, an estimated 22 million tonnes of CO_2 could be released per year.

UNEP also conducted a screening of the potential projects contained in the NDF for CDM potential. A number of projects were identified, including afforestation and reforestation, hydroelectric and wind energy development, natural and bio-gas development, and solar power. Project examples are listed in Annex A.

In order for Afghanistan to benefit from the CDM, it will need to declare voluntary participation and establish a focal point: a National CDM Authority. While the private sector will

ENVIRONMENTAL GOVERNANCE

be the primary project developers, the government will have a fundamental role to play in approving CDM projects, assessing project verification reports and governing the sale and transfer of certified emission reductions (CERs) units. An important restriction that must be recognized is that CDM funding cannot come from a diversion of official development assistance (ODA) funds. Cooperation mechanisms between the various government ministries, local authorities and the private sector will also be a prerequisite.

■ Regional environmental cooperation

There are numerous environmental issues and resources in Afghanistan that will require a transboundary approach to management. Examples include water sharing in the Helmand and Amu Darya basins, forest management in the eastern provinces, and protected areas in the Wakhan Corridor and Sistan basin. While negotiations took place between Iran and Afghanistan on the sharing of the Helmand River, the resulting agreement was not formally ratified by Afghanistan due to political instability. Two important agreements were, however, made on the transboundary management of the Amu Darya River: the 1946 *frontier agreement between Afghanistan and the former Soviet Union*, and the 1958 *treaty concerning the regime to the Soviet-Afghan frontier*. These agreements established an international commission to deal with the use and quality of frontier water resources, but no progress has been made on institutions for transboundary management due to the recent conflict.

High-level talks on transboundary environmental management have restarted within the framework of ECO – the Economic Cooperation Organization. ECO is an intergovernmental organization established in 1985 by Iran, Pakistan and Turkey for the purpose of sustainable socio-economic development of the member states. In 1992, ECO was expanded to include the Islamic State of Afghanistan, Republic of Azerbaijan, Republic of Kazakhstan, Kyrgyz Republic, Republic of Tajikistan, Turkmenistan and Republic of Uzbekistan. The first ECO ministerial meeting on the environment was held in Tehran on 15 December 2002. Participants agreed on the Tehran Declaration on Cooperation Among ECO Member States as well as a plan of action. Topics included harmonization of environmental standards, environmentally sound technologies, urban environmental management, improving Environmental Impact Assessment systems, eco-tourism, establishment of an ECO Environmental College and developing an ECO Environmental Fund. Support was also pledged to Afghanistan in developing and strengthening its environmental authorities and in establishing an Environmental Protection Agency.

Education

The Ministry of Education, with UN and NGO support, has begun the process of rebuilding the education system, including school construction and repair, curriculum reform and teacher training. Initial results from the back-to-school campaign to return 1.78 million children to school by March 2002 suggest nearly twice the expected number returned. Kabul University also reopened its doors and provided entrance examinations to 20 000 students.

■ Environmental awareness

Environmental education does not currently exist at the primary, secondary or university levels. Overall, public understanding of the links between environmental degradation, health and human livelihoods is very low. There are also few teachers with adequate training on environmental topics, and no professional development programmes.

The Ministry of Education recognizes the needs to incorporate basic environmental education into the primary and secondary school curriculum. Technical assistance is required to achieve this goal.

The University of Kabul envisions the day when a basic course on environment will be compulsory for graduation. It is also interested in developing specific technical courses on environmental management and rehabilitation within its Faculty of Agriculture. The Environment Conservation Centre for Afghanistan (ECFA) has been established within the university. With adequate funding, the centre would like to establish a volunteer association for environmental protection. ECFA also aims to develop environmental education materials for school curricula and radio, collect and distribute environmental information, and lobby for environmental rights.

Public participation in decision-making

Although the Transitional Authority is currently in the process of developing a new constitution, a legal framework, and the necessary institutional structures for governance, the role of the public has not been well defined. There are at present no clear mechanisms for public participation, nor is the public able to voice its concerns through any consultative forum. The country's media are functioning at a very low level, and therefore do not yet offer a significant channel for expression of ideas and issues. At the local level, community interests are often represented by the ruling factions and traditional decision-making structures suffer from a lack of transparency. The role of women is also very weak.

Afghanistan was virtually isolated from the international environmental community during the past two decades. As a result, opportunities for Afghanistan to benefit from new approaches to public participation in environmental management were limited. Although many NGOs tried to act in the interest of the environment, financial resources were often insufficient to meet the vast needs. In addition, NGO activities were often discouraged in favour of government-led implementation.

During the period of conflict, many people with professional qualifications were removed from positions of authority or excluded from participating in government. As a result many individuals remained active by shifting into non-governmental organizations. UNEP observed that many NGOs, such as DACAAR (Danish Committee for Aid to Afghan Refugees), MADERA (a European NGO), Afghan Aid, ARC (Afghan Relief Committee), IRC (International Rescue Committee), AREA (Agency for Rehabilitation and Energy Conservation in Afghanistan) and SEA (Save the Environment Afghanistan), have strong environmental programmes with high levels of training and competency for project implementation.

An umbrella organization known as ACBAR (Agency Coordinating Body for Afghanistan) has also been established to coordinate NGO activities. It has established a resource and information centre which collects and disseminates information to the UN, NGOs, donors and the Transitional Authority.

6 Recommendations

The past two decades of conflict in Afghanistan have prevented effective implementation of previous environmental management and conservation strategies. Conflict has degraded management capacity, destroyed infrastructure, and hindered agricultural activities. These effects, coupled with three to four years of drought affecting most of the country, have caused serious and widespread land and resource degradation, including lowered water tables, desiccation of wetlands, deforestation and widespread loss of vegetative cover, erosion, and loss of wildlife populations. These problems are compounded by the increasing numbers of people who are being displaced due to insecurity arising from degraded environments and loss of livelihoods.

The significant lack of effective environmental management and the extensive environmental damage and degradation that has been detailed in the previous chapters is increasing human vulnerability to natural disasters. With the widespread loss of forest and vegetation cover, fragile soils are now exposed to both wind and water erosion. The first heavy rains could wash away existing soils from steep slopes and lead to massive landslides. Both scenarios could reduce or destroy land productivity. Without vegetation to act as a sponge to absorb rainwater, extensive flooding is also likely to occur, eroding both river channels and key agricultural lands downstream. Sedimentation of irrigation canals and river basins will further exacerbate the situation.

With the return of hundreds of thousands of refugees, additional pressures will be added to both urban environmental infrastructures and to demands on natural resources. Without assistance from the international community in developing sustainable livelihoods, desperation could result in increased environmental degradation, including further loss of forest cover, overgrazing, uncoordinated water use and unsustainable dry land cultivation.

The trends are clear and Afghanistan currently faces three different kinds of environmental scarcity[100].

- The *supply* of environmental goods and services is decreasing due to degradation, overuse and mismanagement.

- The *demand* for environmental goods and services is increasing with high levels of population growth and millions of returning refugees.

- *Access* to environmental goods and services is unequal owing to ongoing civil disorder and power imbalances.

International experience has demonstrated that further increases in environmental scarcity could cause an influx of millions of refugees into urban areas or neighbouring countries, causing increased tensions and continued instability, and setting the stage for renewed conflicts.

With the restoration of national governance comes the opportunity to develop a realistic plan for remedial action and to expand national capacity toward sustainable use and restoration of the country's natural resources. Without such planning and management of resources, it will be difficult for humanitarian aid and development efforts to succeed in the long run, and the potential for the environmental crisis to deepen with subsequent political instability and upheaval, is a serious possibility.

In order to address the environmental issues identified by the UNEP assessment, a series of cross-cutting, sector-based and site-specific recommendations are given below. Where possible the recommendations have been divided into immediate actions that can be taken to reduce risks to human health or to arrest environmental degradation, and longer-term suggestions related to planning, capacity building and institutional development.

Responsibility for implementing these recommendations lies with the government and people of Afghanistan. The newly established Ministry of Irrigation, Water Resources and Environment must play a critical role in designing and preparing new laws, standards and activities to address the environmental management, protection and rehabilitation needs of the country. This should occur in full cooperation with the key sector ministries responsible for implementation including Agriculture and Animal Husbandry, Public Health, Rural Development, Urban Development and Housing, Water and Power, and Mines and Industry. Mechanisms for enforcement must be developed between the various sector ministries and their partners at the central, regional and local levels. The basic rule of law and constitution must be followed at all times. The Ministry of Irrigation, Water Resources and Environment will have a key role to play in monitoring compliance with the new environmental regulations and in issuing environmental permits according to prescribed standards.

It is important also to recognize that long-term improvements in the environmental conditions of the country cannot be achieved without strong regional cooperation, and sustained technical and financial assistance from the international community.

Cross-cutting environmental management recommendations

For the government of Afghanistan to address effectively the great environmental challenges faced by the country, strong and well-equipped environmental authorities are needed to guide and design new environmental management tools and policies, as well as monitor the implementation of protection and restoration projects. In all cases, ecological limits should be used to define appropriate use levels and limits for human activities. The following recommendations are cross-cutting in nature and responsibility for pursuing them will fall on the Ministry of Irrigation, Water Resources and Environment in cooperation with other key ministries such as Agriculture and Animal Husbandry, Public Health, Urban Development and Housing, and Rural Development.

■ Environmental legislation and enforcement

Environmental legislation forms the cornerstone of an effective institutional framework for environmental protection, sustainable use and rehabilitation. Legislation must establish clear management authority in each area, provide guidance on local implementation, and establish measures for monitoring and enforcement. The following actions should be undertaken in the immediate future to improve the legislative base for environmental management in Afghanistan:

1. Recognize environmental rights in the national constitution: There are already positive indications that provisions on environmental rights will be entrenched in Afghanistan's new constitution. These efforts should be further supported and the fundamental right of all citizens to a healthy and clean environment should be recognized in the supreme law of the land. This would empower citizens to take action against violations of this right through administrative and judicial procedures.

2. Consult stakeholders on the framework environmental law: The Ministry of Irrigation, Water Resources and Environment, in collaboration with the Ministry of Justice, has initiated the process of developing a draft environmental framework law. This provides a significant opportunity to develop effective institutional structures for inter-ministry collaboration and cooperation, as well as for public consultation. All sectoral ministries with environmental responsibilities should be consulted in finalizing the framework environmental law.

3. Introduce routine use of Environmental Impact Assessment: Use EIAs as a means to promote sustainable development by integrating environmental considerations into the actions proposed by different sectors. In the medium to long term, EIAs can save costs (for example, for clean-up, or preventing environmental or ecological disasters).

4. Strengthen enforcement mechanisms: The judicial system is currently weak and poorly equipped to deal with environmental litigation. Current efforts by the Judicial Commission to improve the rule of law should include provisions for the enforcement of new environmental laws. Training programmes are needed urgently to build knowledge and strengthen the capacities of judges and magistrates, as well as that of public prosecutors, to deal with environmental issues. In addition, the role of police and customs officers in the enforcement of national environmental laws and international agreements needs to be recognized. Collaboration between ministries with environmental responsibilities and the Ministry of Justice will be required.

5. Establish participatory processes: Without the involvement of citizens in decisions on the management of natural resources, the integrity of the legal framework may be compromised. To ensure adequate participation, build into the constitution appropriate consultation processes with all stakeholders at both national and local levels. The village *shura/jirga* and mosque have traditionally held important roles in local decision-making, and this role should be recognized.

6. Introduce environmental permits: Provision should be made within new legislation for the development of environmental quality standards and licenses covering water, air, soil, chemicals, and hazardous wastes. Such procedures should be overseen by national or local environmental inspectors with powers to inspect, monitor and enforce compliance with legal standards.

7. Employ economic incentives: Consider the use of economic and fiscal incentives or instruments to encourage compliance with prescribed standards and environmental regulations. Such incentives may include tax rebates, subsidies, research grants, and reduction or exemption from import tax or duty on 'green' equipment.

8. Share information: While multiple ministries will be engaged in the collection of environmental information, a mechanism will be needed for information sharing and consolidation into a central database. The public should have access to all information collected.

9. Coordinate environmental monitoring: Environmental monitoring should be coordinated through a central point, although actual collection of data is likely to remain the responsibility of multiple ministries, perhaps with an increasing role at the local level. The primary goal of central coordination is to ensure availability of data to support sound decision-making at a national level. This also implies the use of standardized tools and methods for collecting, analyzing and interpreting data. Satellite images and repeat photography can be effective tools for monitoring environmental change.

10. Develop 'soft' enforcement measures: In addition to strengthening traditional means of enforcement, there is also a need to develop alternative, 'softer' means of law enforcement. This includes the use of positive incentives and voluntary agreements. The latter are likely to be vital for securing environmental commitments from local communities and the expanding private sector. Community-based resource management, monitoring and enforcement will also play a critical role in the future management of the natural resource base.

11. Develop environmental budgeting: The Ministry of Irrigation, Water Resources and Environment should, in cooperation with other relevant sector ministries, develop an environmental budget on an annual basis in cooperation with the Ministry of Finance. The budget should be used as a planning tool, outlining progress made in the previous year, priority needs, and required costs.

12. Debate multilateral environmental agreements: The draft constitution should include a provision requiring the government to present any environmental convention under consideration to parliament for due debate and authorization. Such debate should also provide opportunity for relevant NGOs, professional organizations and academic institutions to participate and share views.

■ Capacity building for environmental management

For the Afghanistan Transitional Authority to design, implement and enforce effective environmental laws and policies, capacity building for environmental management must be undertaken in the Ministry of Irrigation, Water Resources and Environment as well as in each of the key sector ministries. Priorities include the following steps and measures.

13. Provide basic infrastructure:

(a) Environmental offices within each ministry need basic furniture (desks, chairs and filing cabinets, etc.), stationery, electricity and wiring for modern telecommunications equipment such as telephones, faxes, and computers with internet and e-mail systems and other appropriate software.

(b) Information and communication resources need to include a library or documentation centre from which staff can access environmental, technical and legal material.

(c) Transportation facilities are required to enable staff to carry out their ministry's mandate. Recurrent maintenance and fuel costs will also need to be included.

14. Provide professional training: An immediate requirement is staff training in the areas of literacy, numeracy, accounting and computing skills. Professional training is then required in a range of environmental management fields, including budget and project development and management; environmental law development, implementation and enforcement; setting of environmental standards and monitoring compliance; use of economic instruments; and involvement of environmental stakeholders.

15. Strengthen the mandate of the Ministry of Irrigation, Water Resources and Environment: A clear mandate should be provided to this Ministry to conduct the following measures:

(a) Develop and disseminate general and specific environmental policy goals to guide officials in the execution of their duty, and inform public opinion. These goals also need to be communicated to the donor community.

(b) Develop a strategic plan that prioritizes drafting of new environmental legislation based upon the hierarchy of policies, laws and regulations that need to be addressed.

(c) Establish specific units responsible for environmental impact assessment, international environmental treaties and transboundary agreements, project development proposals, environmental information, development of legislation, and inter-ministry coordination.

(d) Involve the public in the development of policies, strategies, action plans and environmental laws.

(e) Scale down the present unfunded plan for high staffing levels to a more realistic level. Aim for a small tightly focused team with the flexibility and skills required to address the most urgent needs during the reconstruction phase.

(f) With reference to the decisions of the Economic Cooperation Organization (ECO) ministerial meeting on environment in December 2002, establish an Environmental Protection Agency.

16. Introduce an inter-ministerial coordination mechanism: Given the cross-cutting nature of environmental management, allocation of environmental responsibilities is currently divided between a number of ministries. An inter-ministerial coordination mechanism is needed to provide a forum to debate cross-cutting environmental issues, coordinate environmental policy, use comparative advantages and avoid duplication of effort. The body should either be convened by the Ministry of Irrigation, Water Resources and the Environment, or by the President's office. In the event of a dispute, a means to obtain final arbitration at Cabinet, Vice-Presidential or Presidential level should be included.

17. Establish inter-agency technical committees: Inter-agency technical committees or authorities are needed to deal with technical environmental issues that cross-cut ministry mandates. Committees are required immediately for:

> Water Resources

> Land Resources

> Waste Management

> Protected Areas

> Environmental Conventions and the Clean-Development Mechanism.

18. Adopt decentralized, community-based management approaches: Afghan villages have a long history and strong vested interest in managing their natural resources on a sustainable basis. However, pastures, forests, water resources and wildlife populations are still being managed as common property resources but without the traditional constraints that once prevented over-exploitation. Solutions relevant to local communities that are based upon local community traditions and practices offer the best way forward. However, a return to the 'former ways' is no longer possible, given the current degraded state of the resource base, population and migration stresses, and other international pressures. Strong central regulations are clearly needed to respond to these new challenges, coupled with a partnership role for local communities in implementation and enforcement. Communities will also require adequate technical support from the central government in order to rehabilitate degraded land, develop land-use plans, and balance resource use with conservation.

19. Strengthen regional cooperation: Management of transboundary environmental issues, such as water resources, forests and protected areas, will require increased regional cooperation. Mechanisms need to be established to manage sustainable use, harmonize environmental standards, share information and best practice, address illegal trade, and settle disputes. The first ministerial meeting on environment of the Economic Cooperation

Organization (ECO) in December 2002, is an important first step at strengthening regional environmental cooperation. The agreements made at this meeting should form an important component of government policy and swift efforts should be taken towards implementation by the relevant Ministries and stakeholders.

20. Join other international environmental processes: For the last two decades, Afghanistan has been largely excluded from the international environmental community and related processes. Opportunities for reconnecting with the following international environmental processes should be carefully considered: Environment for Europe (EfE), International Year of Freshwater, World Water Forum, World Forestry Congress, World Parks Congress, World Solar Congress, and the Bishkek Mountain Framework.

■ Environment and job creation

With chronic unemployment across Afghanistan, the Transitional Authority is developing immediate cash or food-for-work projects that benefit people most in need. It is important to recognize that environmental restoration, conservation and management efforts can create numerous employment opportunities when coupled with labour-intensive methods. The following recommendations should be taken into account by the Ministry of Irrigation, Water Resources and Environment and key sector Ministries to maximize job creation in the environment sector.

21. Support labour-based rehabilitation projects: Whenever possible, environmental rehabilitation projects should be undertaken with labour-intensive methods and cash-for-work programmes. Immediate activities might include reforestation, cleaning and repair of water infrastructure, installation of septic tanks, materials recovery and metals recycling, manual pest control, waste clean-up and wildlife surveys. All projects should be carefully monitored and adaptive management practices applied.

22. Prioritize hiring of Afghan professionals and staff: When possible, UN agencies and donors should give priority to hiring of Afghan professionals and staff members. When needed, appropriate training should be provided to supplement or compliment existing skills.

23. Afghanistan Conservation Corps: The proposal to establish an Afghan Conservation Corps with former combatants could be an important tool in national reforestation efforts while at the same time providing thousands of jobs for vulnerable people. However, it needs to be carefully planned and implemented in order to ensure activities are conducted in a socially and ecologically appropriate way. Before any trees are planted, ecological surveys should be conducted to identify and prioritize areas that have the greatest potential for successful reforestation and recovery. This should take into account soil suitability and water availability, land ownership, and the ability to protect the site from grazing, dry land cultivation, erosion, fire, insects and flooding. Local communities must also support the project and obtain long-term benefits that help to improve livelihoods. Projects must also be supported by national forest policies and participants must be provided with adequate technical training.

24. Transform and add value to products from natural resources: Products from natural resources should be transformed as much as possible within Afghanistan to maximize employment opportunities. To achieve this goal, appropriate technical assistance and financial mechanisms will be required from the international community, NGOs and the Afghanistan Transitional Authority.

25. Maximize economic benefits from nature tourism: Protected areas can generate sources of foreign income from international nature tourism. Opportunities for establishing

6

fee-based park entry permits for international visitors should be explored, and overnight accommodation and visitor facilities developed in order to lengthen stays. Local communities must support and participate in the management of the protected area and receive financial benefits from the sale of crafts and food, and the rental of guides, equipment, accommodation and local transport. Local communities should also be trained in minimizing visitor impacts in protected areas and in monitoring environmental change and wildlife populations.

■ Environmental planning

26. Clarify land tenure and begin land-use planning: The first and continuing priority for rebuilding Afghanistan is to maintain natural and agricultural ecosystems in order to sustain human livelihoods and biological diversity. In order to achieve this goal, the current state of degradation and carrying capacity of the resource base must be assessed in order to plan a comprehensive programme of ecological restoration and sustainable use. A parallel effort must also establish a process for clarifying and mapping land ownership and tenure. Results should be used to jointly plan settlements, agricultural activities and industrial development that respect ecological limits, conditions and natural boundaries.

27. Develop a National Environmental Action Plan (NEAP): Afghanistan faces a huge number of environmental problems that include poor freshwater quality, lowering water tables, disappearing vegetative cover, and waste disposal. While all of these require action, it is important to prioritize immediate goals and to understand the linkages between each issue. The government of Afghanistan should develop a National Environmental Action Plan (NEAP) that will recognize the most acute problems and development opportunities, identify potential solutions, give clear targets, and lay out strategies to reach those targets. The NEAP should take into account the 'polluter pays' principle and the precautionary approach of environmental management. The plan should also serve as a basis for the development of policies and legislation affecting the different environmental sectors. Development of the NEAP should be guided by the Ministry of Irrigation, Water Resources and Environment in close cooperation with other relevant ministries. The drafting process should also involve NGOs, scientific institutions and other stakeholders.

28. Prepare emergency response and contingency plans: Due to widespread and long-term environmental degradation, vulnerabilities to natural disasters, such as drought and flooding, are increasing. The Department of Emergency and Disaster Assistance (under the President's office) needs urgent assistance to increase the country's state of preparedness and capacity to manage environmental disasters and emergencies. Plans must address specifically the need to engage in prevention, early warning and mitigation measures.

■ Environmental impact assessment procedures

The Afghanistan Transitional Authority has expressed a strong interest in developing a comprehensive EIA process. In the absence of enforceable EIA legislation, interim measures should already be taken to conduct EIAs including the following:

29. Apply EIAs across the board: The Transitional Authority should establish clear criteria and a comprehensive procedure for conducting EIAs. As an interim measure a decree or other similar instrument should be issued insisting that UN agencies, banks, bilateral donors and international NGOs use their own established EIA guidelines and procedures for all programmes and projects proposed or undertaken in Afghanistan.

30. Establish an inter-ministerial EIA task force: An EIA Task Force, including representation from key ministries with environmental responsibilities, could be co-chaired by

Post-Conflict Environmental Assessment

the Ministry of Irrigation, Water Resources and Environment and the Afghan Aid Coordination Authority. It should identify key projects requiring EIA, approve the scope and approach of each EIA, review EIA reports, make recommendations to decision-making authorities, and ensure that public involvement has taken place. It should also initiate work on the development of a simplified EIA procedure for the private sector and local non-governmental organizations, to be used in the interim period until the appropriate legal EIA infrastructure is in place.

31. Establish a dedicated EIA Unit: An EIA Unit established within the Ministry of Irrigation, Water Resources and Environment could act as the secretariat for the EIA Task Force and begin the development of EIA legislation. The unit would require a legal specialist and expertise in natural resource use, environmental engineering, and socio-economic aspects.

32. Apportion EIA costs: The costs of an EIA study should be borne by the project's proponents, and hence included in the overall costs of the project. The project should also cover the costs of any mitigation and environmental management measures suggested by an EIA. Costs associated with reviewing EIA findings should be met by the EIA Unit and the EIA Task Force. To some extent these administrative costs could be covered by charging an EIA processing fee (for example, 0.5 per cent of the overall value of the project).

33. Build professional expertise to undertake EIAs: The effectiveness of the EIA process depends on the availability of qualified personnel with the appropriate technical skills and expertise to carry out research, analyses and preparation of EIA reports of sufficient quality to inform decision-making. The quality of technical work also entails availability of baseline data and information on the natural environment. Training is required to build the necessary capacity for these tasks within government ministries and academic institutions. Basic modules should cover project scoping, cost-benefit analyses, environmental mitigation, compliance monitoring, and public participation. Once trained, Afghan experts should be integrated into EIAs carried out on behalf of donors, UN agencies and development banks.

■ Industry and trade

International experience has demonstrated that poorly managed industrial development and trade can lead to significant, long-term social and environmental impacts. Afghanistan has a culturally strong and vigorous private sector but almost no significant industrial development, and limited international trade. The following activities should be conducted in order to integrate environmental considerations into industrial development and trade practices:

34. Develop best environmental practice in the private sector: Industry and private sector developments must be subject to EIAs and relevant regulations. Economic instruments including taxes, permits, and emissions charges should be considered by the Transitional Authority as an important tool in the regulation of the private sector. National planning and environmental authorities should plan industrial development in areas that minimize environmental and health impacts, while at the same time maximizing collective use of pollution control and waste processing services – a practice known as industrial ecology. This would help to ensure that industrial developments are properly sited and compliant with minimal environmental protection requirements. The private sector will need assistance in building capacity for environmental reporting and in the use of environmental management systems. A strategy should be developed to attract the 'right kind' of foreign direct investments that recognize environmental standards and use best available eco-technology.

35. Prevent illegal trade in hazardous waste, raw materials and products: The current state of the Afghan economy and lack of customs control may serve to increase imports of banned toxic chemicals and hazardous wastes, as well as exports of endangered wildlife and illegally harvested timber. Customs regulations and control practices must be upgraded to prevent illegal trade, and customs officers must be properly trained in detecting illegal products.

36. Promote cleaner production: Afghanistan's industrial sector could benefit from the introduction of cleaner production technologies and approaches. This would help to minimize waste generation and pollution emissions, as well as improve energy efficiency. It would also enable companies to cut costs, while at the same time allowing local authorities to reduce expenditure on waste disposal infrastructure and environmental remediation. Training and education of the private sector on new, cleaner production technologies and management practices should be promoted by the international community and the Afghan Ministry of Mines and Industry.

37. Assess privatization impacts: Privatization of environmental goods and services, such as water and energy supplies, should be carefully considered against long-term environmental and social costs. In this regard, the Afghan authorities should draw on the past and recent experience of many developing countries with both positive and negative privatization experience. If some privatization occurs, complementary policies and mechanisms should be developed to mitigate potential social and environmental impacts.

38. Develop and market environmentally friendly products and services: The Transitional Authority, in cooperation with business and industry associations, should promote the development and marketing of environmentally friendly products and services. Programmes, including the introduction of eco-labeling, green product awards, deposit/refund systems, waste minimization and reusable packing should be explored. Trade and market measures should be developed that support these goals.

39. Minimize impacts on food security from new international trade: As Afghanistan reopens its markets to international trade, precautions should be taken by the Transitional Authority to ensure domestic food security is not compromised by excessive export-oriented agricultural production and trade.

40. Diversify the industrial and agricultural production base: To avoid vulnerability from market fluctuations, the Transitional Authority should encourage the industrial and agricultural sectors to maintain a diverse range of products.

41. Transform and add value to primary products for export: Primary products that are destined for export should be transformed as much as possible in Afghanistan so as to maximize export value and employment opportunities. To achieve this goal, appropriate technical assistance and financial mechanisms will be required from the international community, NGOs and the Transitional Authority.

42. Mitigate the potential environmental and social impacts of trade: While international trade opportunities can generate important sources of income, it is essential to acknowledge that international trade pressures can also become a critical driving force in the over-exploitation of natural resources. As a result, measures should be taken to properly mitigate and manage the potential environmental and social impacts of trade. This will also ensure sustainable use of the resource base in the long term.

Post-Conflict Environmental Assessment

■ Public participation, training and environmental education

While the government has a crucial role in creating the structures and processes for sustainable and environmentally sound management and development, implementation will depend heavily on the Afghan people and their organizations. Public participation in discussions and decision-making on environmental issues and management of natural resources requires more heightened levels of awareness and understanding than exist presently within the broad Afghan community. Many of the required immediate and long-term improvements will require the introduction of totally new environmental policies and tools. Therefore, training and capacity building needs in the environmental sector are considerable. International agencies and donors should address the need for environmental management training. The following recommendations are made to improve the knowledge base among the different stakeholders:

43. Establish rights to environmental information and access to justice: In order to promote public participation in decision-making, the Transitional Authority should establish clear legal rights on access to environmental information and justice for environmental matters. Best practice guidelines could be obtained from the 1998 UNECE Aarhus Convention.

44. Improve access to government processes: Measures to address the lack of public access to governmental processes are needed, notably in the forthcoming development of environmental policies such as the framework environmental law, national constitution and EIA legislation.

45. Establish a resource centre for environmental information and best practice: An environmental resource centre should be established by the Ministry of Irrigation, Water Resources and Environment and relevant stakeholders. The centre would collect, organize and distribute to the public and NGO community information on environmental conditions, monitoring results, ongoing programmes and international best practice in environmental management. Such measures would help to build greater environmental awareness and also provide feedback on ongoing conservation or rehabilitation measures. Information should be provided in a way that takes into consideration the diversity of literacy rates and languages spoken in the country.

46. Increase media awareness: The Ministry of Irrigation, Water Resources and Environment should work directly with the press and media to increase their awareness of environmental issues and promote coverage of environmental topics.

47. Develop environmental education materials: All sectors of society will benefit from exposure to environmental education materials, presented in a manner suitable for communities with varied literacy levels, and using at least two Afghan languages. As a first step, simple posters could be developed on basic environmental themes in both urban and rural settings. Given the widespread use of and interest in local radio, opportunities for the delivery of environmental education using this medium should be thoroughly explored. Developing films on environmental problems should also be promoted. Educational films could be shown in rural locations using mobile screens and projection equipment.

48. Develop an environmental education curriculum: There is an urgent need to integrate environmental education into both rural and urban primary and secondary school curricula, as well as in universities. An assessment is needed to identify priorities for curriculum development and to determine the most effective mechanisms for countrywide delivery. Formal methods must be coupled with efforts to reach adult audiences through community-focused adult environmental education. All activities should be coordinated with key stakeholders including NGOs, UNICEF, UNESCO, the Ministry of Education, and the academic community.

49. Train teachers to deliver environmental education: In order to integrate environmental issues into school and university studies, adequate training programmes for teachers are needed. An immediate first step should be the development of guidebooks for teachers. In the longer term, universities should ensure all teachers have mandatory training in basic environmental concepts. Opportunities for international exchange visits should be investigated.

50. Provide environmental training: The government should include environmental themes in the ongoing training programmes of all civil servants and authorities. Training should include an introduction to the key environmental policy principles and management instruments.

51. Inventory traditional ecological knowledge: Afghanistan is a country with a rich tradition of community-based solutions to environmental problems. However, due to the recent conflict, traditional methods of environmental management have fallen out of practice in some areas. An inventory should be conducted of traditional ecological knowledge on environmental management, seeking to identify methods and techniques that could be re-activated to improve environmental management, and/or supplemented with modern practices.

52. Unite environment and religion: Religious leaders should be called upon to promote improved environmental practices at the rural and urban levels. The links between environmental conservation and religious practice should also be emphasized.

Sectoral environmental management recommendations

Sector ministries have been established by the Transitional Authority to take the lead role in implementing programmes and policies covering the traditional environmental sectors such as water, waste, forests, and wildlife. Implementation of the following recommendations rests with these sector ministries, including Agriculture and Animal Husbandry, Public Health, Urban Development and Housing, Water and Power, and Mines and Industry. However, the Ministry of Irrigation, Water Resources and Environment should be a key partner in providing relevant expertise, ensuring best practice is being applied, facilitating project implementation and monitoring results.

■ Water supply

Water is key to the health and well-being of Afghanistan's people, and essential to maintain agricultural productivity – the heart of the Afghan economy. As outlined in the UNICEF sponsored "Kabul Understanding on Water Resource Management and Development in Afghanistan", improved water resource management will, in many regions, be an essential first step in rebuilding rural communities. An important opportunity exists to adopt a model for freshwater management that will serve the people and ecosystems of the country while at the same time benefiting from international best practice. Key responsibilities for improving water resources management lie with the Ministries of Irrigation, Water Resources and Environment, Water and Power, and the envisioned National Water Authority. Immediate actions that can be taken to stop the degradation of water resources and to improve management are given below.

53. Test and monitor water quality: Portable water-testing equipment should be used on key water supplies to regularly test for risks to human health. According to WHO, the critical water-quality parameters to be tested are *Escherichia coli (E. Coli)*, total coliforms and chlorine residual (if chlorination is practiced). These should be supplemented by pH (if chlorination is practiced) and turbidity (if any treatment is effected). Nitrate analyses are also recommended to be included.

54. Identify and eliminate cross-contamination: In order to alleviate the worst effects of poor sanitation, wastewater and water supply officials must begin to routinely coordinate their knowledge and activities in order to repair immediately infrastructure that may be leading to the cross-contamination of water supplies with wastewater.

55. Stop unmanaged deep well drilling: All proposed deep well drilling activities should be stopped immediately until information is collected on possible short- and long-term impacts to shallow wells, *karez* systems and natural wetlands in the area. Possible contamination risks from waste disposal sites and septic tank systems should also be addressed.

56. Protect water supply sources: In order to protect water supplies from cross-contamination and to ensure a long-term safe water supply, it is critically important that sanitary protection zones are established around all existing and new water supply sources. A minimum zone of 30 m should be applied, extending to 300 m wherever possible.

57. Properly equip the water sector:

(a) Despite the considerable efforts of various international organizations, there is still an overwhelming need for equipment to rehabilitate well fields, reservoirs, pumping stations and pipelines. An equally strong need exists for leakage detection equipment, water meters and water level indicators.

(b) Afghanistan's drinking water laboratories are also poorly equipped, and staff lack training in modern methods of drinking water analysis. A fully equipped laboratory should be established at the Ministry of Public Health, and staff trained to perform and analyze drinking water samples.

58. Promote water conservation: UNEP observed that despite drought conditions and lack of supply, water conservation measures are not applied consistently. Furthermore, crops with low water demands are neither used nor promoted during drought years. Public education programmes are needed urgently at both urban and rural levels to improve awareness of water conservation techniques. Immediate assessments are also needed to determine efficiency of water use for different crops in the agricultural sector, opportunities for conservation, and substitute crops during drought years.

In the medium to long term, the following policies and management activities will also be required:

59. Develop a National Water Resources Management Strategy: UNICEF and WWF have taken important steps to develop a sustainable water resource management strategy for Afghanistan[101][102]. These contributions should form a core part of a new national water resources management strategy by the Afghanistan Transitional Authority. At a minimum, the new strategy should focus on the following elements:

(a) Adopting a river basin approach that considers both surface and ground water resources as well as multiple social goals rather than the needs of one sector.

(b) Balancing water needs and considering the most efficient use concerning drinking water, sanitation and wastewater, irrigation and animal husbandry, hydroelectricity, forests, rangelands and wetlands.

(c) Taking measures to regulate storage and release of water in a way that meets the needs of users throughout any given catchment, taking account of the productive potential of different terrain, and without harming the overall integrity of aquatic systems.

(d) Developing national or regional conservation measures in the event of drought.

(e) Conducting a comprehensive inventory of water resources and developing an overall monitoring framework for water quality. This should include relevant water quality standards as well as water quantity, including an early-warning system for drought and flooding.

(f) Activating existing and establishing new agreements for the joint management of transboundary water resources.

(g) Establishing a framework for the protection of water rights and access.

60. Develop a National Water Authority: Responsibilities for water management are fragmented between six ministries: Irrigation, Water Resources and Environment, Water and Power, Urban Development and Housing, Rural Rehabilitation and Development, Agriculture and Animal Husbandry, and Public Health. A high-level National Water Authority is needed to develop a national water resources management strategy, coordinate the activities of all ministries, perform dispute resolution between ministries, monitor progress towards national water goals, and oversee infrastructure developments.

61. Develop groundwater monitoring programmes: These are needed in all of Afghanistan's major cities to provide a basis for proper groundwater management and the development of long-term plans for sustainable drinking water supplies. Such programmes should include descriptions of hydrogeology, drilling of appropriate monitoring wells, determining key hydraulic parameters (for example, through pumping tests), and analyses of water quality and groundwater levels surrounding the various aquifers. A permanent monitoring programme should be put in place in order to determine annual trends in water quality and water levels. All data should be stored and managed for ease of access in decision-making.

62. Promote transboundary water resources management: Many neighbouring countries, including Iran, Pakistan, Tajikistan, Uzbekistan and Turkmenistan, use water resources that originate in Afghanistan. As Afghanistan considers future extraction of these resources, potential impacts on downstream users need to be carefully considered. Afghanistan needs to become a full participant in ongoing transboundary water management processes, and clarify the legal status of previous agreements. Future transboundary water management agreements should be developed. These should include specific provisions for water rights and allocation, dispute resolution mechanisms, compensation for damage in event of overuse, and emergency water management measures during periods of drought.

63. Study the hydrological contributions of glaciers, permanent snowfields and snowfall:

(a) Conduct a technical assessment of the extent of glaciers, permanent snowfields and annual snowfall in Afghanistan, and their contribution to hydrology.

(b) Develop a monitoring and early-warning system for drought, floods, and glacial lake outburst flood (GLOF) events.

(c) Identify both mitigation strategies and disaster response mechanisms.

Post-Conflict Environmental Assessment

64. Consider impacts of climate change:

(a) Global climate change processes may lead to significant alteration of present snow and rainfall patterns. Attempts should be made to assess the probable direction and magnitude of such change, and address possible effects in planning a national water development strategy (for instance, by increasing water storage capacity).

(b) Within such a strategy consider the creation of a climate monitoring programme to document changes that can then be applied to adaptive management schemes. This would include monitoring precipitation, humidity, temperature and snow cover.

(c) Warming of glacial areas may lead to increases in GLOF events. Risk analyses of such events should be conducted, and vulnerable areas monitored for early-warning detection.

■ Waste

Management of solid and liquid waste is one of Afghanistan's most serious environmental problems, with direct implications for human health. Already stressed systems could worsen with rapid population growth, increasing urbanization and industrial development. There is an urgent need for the Afghan government to develop waste management policies and initiatives for the entire life cycle of waste – from consumer behaviour to final disposal. Policies should be based on the 'polluter pays' principle. While government must set the national targets and regulations, as well as assign ministerial responsibilities, it should delegate implementation of waste procedures to municipalities and industry. The Ministries of Urban Development and Housing, Mines and Industry, and Irrigation, Water Resources and Environment will have key roles to play, together with the Ministry of Public Health. Immediate steps that can be taken to reduce human health risks from inadequate waste management practices are given below.

65. Segregate and properly dispose of medical waste: Medical waste should be segregated and properly disposed of onsite at hospitals using best practices in health care waste management. The international community should consider building capacity in the health sector and the provision of suitable technology to facilitate the safe management and disposal of medical waste. The production of medical waste by small clinics and individual private households also needs to be addressed.

66. Properly equip the waste management sector: Many steps have already been taken to improve urban waste collection by partnerships involving international organizations, NGOs and national and municipal authorities. However, further assistance is urgently required in the purchase of basic equipment, starting with suitable trucks, high-temperature incinerators, waste transfer equipment, bulldozers, shovels and other equipment. To ensure proper use, projects that supply technology should ensure that correct training is also provided.

67. Identify pollution hotspots: Public facilities or industrial sites posing significant risks to human health from air, soil or water pollution should be designated as pollution hotspots. Relevant environmental parameters should be monitored and the public informed about possible risks to human health. Options for reducing risks, including access restrictions, relocation, or permanent closure, should be assessed and immediate action taken.

In the medium to long term, the following policies and management activities will also be required:

68. Develop a National Strategy for Waste Management: While current waste loads are not high, increasing affluence and industrial development will generate increased waste streams. A strategy is needed to prioritize waste management investments, and to increase compliance with waste laws. The strategy should:

(a) Divide responsibilities for waste management between the central and municipal governments and the private sector.

(b) Consider policies that will promote the re-use or recycling of materials, and minimize the use of packaging.

(c) Consider options for implementing a standardized system of re-usable food and beverage containers, coupled with the development of a depot/refund/sanitization system.

(d) Consider options for avoiding or minimizing the production of hazardous wastes, as well as for the safe storage, handling and treatment of waste products.

(e) Develop technologies for onsite incineration of medical waste.

(f) Develop guidelines for landfill site selection and management targets, including fire prevention, access restrictions, gas and leachate management and groundwater protection.

(g) Develop a system to segregate inert material from ordinary municipal waste in order to reduce the amount of landfill area used and cut fuel costs and truck emissions. Options include establishing waste transfer stations near the city where soil and inert matter can be screened out of the waste matrix, or locating an extraction screen at the waste disposal site.

69. Expand wastewater treatment in all cities and industrial sites: A proper assessment is needed to determine the cost and appropriateness of implementing sewer systems and wastewater treatment technologies in Afghanistan's cities. This assessment should be carried out on a city-by-city basis, supported by the international community. However, all new industrial sites should contain wastewater treatment facilities.

70. Use septic tanks as temporary solutions: As a temporary solution to wastewater management needs, septic tanks can often provide urgently needed improvements on an interim basis.

71. Compost wastewater sludge: Opportunities for converting wastewater sludge into fertilizers should be investigated thoroughly.

■ Hazardous wastes and chemicals

Unregulated use of chemicals and the production of hazardous wastes can present extremely serious, yet often invisible, threats to human and environmental health. Stockpiles of out-of-date or obsolete chemicals or toxic wastes pose a particular risk from deterioration and leakage into soil and groundwater, requiring the need for costly remediation. Unfortunately, limited information is currently available on the threats to human and environmental health posed by poor management of chemicals. The Ministries of Public Health, Mines and Industry, and Irrigation, Water Resources and Environment will have key roles to play in regulating and managing the production of hazardous wastes and chemicals. In order to understand and minimize current risks, the following short-term actions should be implemented.

72. Investigate chemical storage sites: A previous assessment conducted by the World Conservation Union (IUCN)[103] in 1991 reported nearly 7 000 metric tonnes of the persistent, toxic and carcinogenic pesticide BHC (Benzene Hexachloride, also known as Lindane) were being stored in five sites in Mazar-I-Sharif, Pul-I-Khomri, Aibak, Kunduz and Khulum. While no information was available on the location of these sites, a national inventory should be conducted to determine the location, type, quantity and risks posed by existing chemical storage sites across the country. 'Hotspot' sites posing immediate risks to human and environmental health should be identified and remediation strategies developed.

73. Minimize pesticide use: Current efforts towards prevention of pest outbreaks and the introduction of integrated pest management and biological control are positive steps towards reducing the use of pesticides and should be further supported. Given existing levels of unemployment, the use of manual labour should always be given primary consideration when developing pest control measures. Booklets with instructions and guidelines on the safe use, handling and storage of pesticides are required for broad distribution.

74. Monitor pesticides in the environment: Immediate steps should be taken to begin monitoring pesticide residues in air, soil and water and on food products in order to evaluate potential human health and environmental risks. The results should be reported publicly in order to raise awareness and encourage people to take proper precautions during use.

In the medium to long term, the following policies and management activities will also be required:

75. Adopt a strict chemicals policy:

(a) A management authority is needed for classifying hazardous wastes, as well as for dealing with production, treatment, handling and storage standards and procedures.

(b) Policy, legislation and management measures are urgently required for better import and export controls of chemicals such as agricultural pesticides and biocides.

(c) Past experiences have revealed obsolete chemicals are sometimes provided to developing countries as humanitarian aid, or sold for below market prices. The environmental and public health risks of using banned, expired or obsolete chemicals can be high and should be carefully considered.

(d) Special provisions are needed to deal with the production, management and storage of radioactive wastes (for example, from hospitals).

(e) Clear procedures are needed on responses to chemical emergencies, as well as legal clarification over liabilities for clean-up and remediation.

76. Plan for management of hazardous and industrial wastes: With the rebirth of industry will come the production of various hazardous and industrial wastes. The government will need to develop a strict policy for industrial and hazardous waste minimization, as well as standards for transportation, safe handling, storage and treatment. Monitoring of potential exposure risks to humans and the environment should be conducted where hazardous or industrial wastes are produced. Technical assistance could be available from the Basel Convention if Afghanistan were to ratify this treaty. Discharge of industrial or hazardous wastes into the environment should be strictly controlled.

77. Investigate war-related chemical damage: In a post-conflict situation there may be claims or reports of the chemical or radiological hazards arising from weapons used during

6

the conflict, from the infrastructure destroyed, or from collateral damage. Since the side-effects of warfare can have negative effects on both human health and the environment, government officials should always make a full and proper investigation into such claims, supported when needed by the international community and relevant UN agencies.

■ Open woodlands

Open woodlands are extremely valuable as a source of fuelwood, construction materials and for wildlife habitat. Formerly widespread in Afghanistan, this vegetation has in most places been heavily degraded. Excess collection of fuelwood and nuts, grazing pressure and conversion to dry land cultivation have led to severe loss of tree cover and regeneration is minimal. The Ministries of Agriculture and Animal Husbandry and Irrigation, Water Resources and Environment will be important partners in addressing woodland management, conservation and protection. The following urgent actions will be needed to ensure existing woodlands are used in sustainable ways, and that degraded woodland areas are restored.

78. Undertake immediate soil stabilization measures: With the onset of new rains, the current risks of soil erosion are high due to the loss of forest cover and vegetation from drought and overgrazing. Immediate soil stabilization measures should be taken in vulnerable areas to prevent large-scale erosion. This requires a combined approach of reducing grazing pressure in areas prone to erosion, and facilitating rapid regeneration of vegetation cover.

79. Begin community-based reforestation: In areas where complete and extensive deforestation has already taken place, community-based reforestation combined with grazing restrictions will be needed. In the immediate future, surveys will be required to classify the deforested areas according to restoration and regeneration potential. The limited financing that is available should be maximized by focusing on areas with the highest regeneration potential. Areas that are already facing extreme degradation probably do not merit such investment. Restoration should also be prioritized in areas prone to erosion. Once classified, a combination of three options for technical interventions should be considered:

(a) Return the landscape to its original woodland condition using a combination of intensive reforestation efforts and natural regeneration. Strategic pockets of natural forest could be intensively rehabilitated, reaching reproductive capacity in 15 years. These pockets would then provide seed stock for the natural regeneration of adjacent areas. This approach might take up to 50 years to re-establish and regenerate woodland cover.

(b) Replant the area with tree species that could supply alternative sources of income, including fruit-bearing trees, high-yielding nut trees such as pistachios, and trees such as poplar for building materials or fuelwood. This intervention should be designed so that people can shift from reliance on grazing to these alternative income sources. This would help to reduce grazing pressure in remaining woodland areas, and promote natural regeneration.

(c) Restore the area as a managed pasture. Expansion of pasture areas could help to reduce current grazing pressure in existing woodlands. However, communities must agree to move existing livestock to restored areas and not simply increase livestock populations.

80. Reinstate a community-based forest warden system: The former system of community-based forest wardens to monitor land-use activities and impose fines or warnings was effective in the past and should be reinstated and strengthened.

Post-Conflict Environmental Assessment

81. Allocate woodlands to communities: Consideration should be given to the allocation of woodlands to specific communities in order to overcome the problems associated with common-property resources. Communities would be responsible for maintaining the productive capacity of the trees while exclusively benefiting from nut production and limited fuelwood harvesting.

82. Employ grazing management and rotation systems: Community-based rotational grazing schemes should be developed to ensure that grazing pressure is lifted from a sequence of natural woodland areas in order to achieve significant seedling survival. Assessments are also required to determine the carrying capacity of various pasturelands for grazing, taking into account climatic variability and other ecological needs, such as vegetation cover for soil stabilization as well as forest regeneration.

In the medium to long term, the following policies and management activities will also be required:

83. Establish community-based woodlots: Taking land ownership and use rights into consideration, village woodlots for tree nurseries and the planting of fast-growing trees such as poplar for fuelwood and construction should be established. Combined with education programmes and appropriate incentives, this could alleviate some of the pressure on remaining natural woodlands.

84. Establish woodland management legislation: Legislation should be developed to provide a framework for sustainable management of woodlands. Such legislation should cover the regulation of nut and fuelwood harvesting, grazing management, and dry land cultivation. The *shule* system for the regulation of pistachio harvesting needs to be revised to ensure a small proportion of nuts is left to promote seedling regeneration.

85. Establish seed banks: Identify possible sources of desirable production traits and genetic diversity, and collect and maintain adequate material off-site, including the creation of seed banks.

86. Establish woodland protected areas: None of the remaining woodland ecosystems are contained within existing or proposed protected areas. Options for the establishment of a single large protected area, several small nature reserves, and genetic reserves, as well as buffer zones around protected areas, should be considered in order to protect biodiversity and retain examples of original land cover. All protection measures should be conducted with the cooperation and support of local communities.

87. Develop alternative incomes: In order to reduce grazing pressures in the long term, alternative livelihood opportunities are needed for generating incomes. Intensively managed orchards and medicinal plant nurseries may provide such opportunities.

■ Eastern conifer forests

Intense and uncontrolled logging of Afghanistan's eastern conifer forests, especially for deodar cedar, is having a severe impact on forest area and condition. The Ministries of Agriculture and Animal Husbandry and Irrigation, Water Resources and Environment will be important partners in addressing the management, conservation and protection of these forests. While vestiges of the original forests still exist, the following urgent measures are needed to avoid losing the remaining forest cover.

88. Rebuild community control and government influence: Develop and progressively implement a clear strategy for rebuilding community control and government influence in the northeast provinces, aiming to restrict the influence of timber traders, clarify ownership and management responsibilities and increase opportunities for sustainable forest and resource management.

89. Improve transboundary cooperation: The government of Pakistan has an important role to play in stopping the illegal deforestation of conifer forests in Afghanistan. Measures should include import controls, improved border management, and penalties for Pakistani companies found with illegal Afghan timber. Discussions on transboundary cooperation for forest conservation should begin immediately. The international community could also assist by identifying key export markets for Afghan timber and increasing worldwide pressure against illegal importation of Afghan timber.

90. Introduce a timber cooperative: Develop a government-led timber cooperative that could purchase timber directly from communities at fair-market prices, for processing and sale within Afghanistan. Strict management and incentive systems will need to be developed to limit extraction to sustainable levels and to promote regeneration. Some revenues could also be channeled to communities as compensation for establishing protected areas.

91. Seek 'win-win' outcomes in the use of 'Green Forces': The proposal by the Ministry of Agriculture and Animal Husbandry to use 'Green Forces' to control timber extraction and enforce the timber ban should be implemented carefully to achieve 'win-win' outcomes both for the government and for local communities. In some countries, 'Green Force' models have done more harm than good, and care needs to be taken to prevent tension and renewed conflicts. Green Forces could be made available to help communities enforce forest management agreements where they are threatened by powerful outside interests. Enforcement should be conducted according to the rule of law and be consistent with forest legislation, while at the same time respecting community traditions and local needs.

92. Control road access to forests: Access to forest resources as a result of road building has been a contributory factor in deforestation. Thus, all future road construction projects need to consider the potential impacts on forests. UN agencies and NGOs need to be sensitized to the links between road construction and deforestation. EIAs should be carried out on all future road developments affecting conifer forests and access management plans developed with input from local communities.

93. Estimate future timber demands: An overall strategy for obtaining adequate timber supplies to meet reconstruction needs has not been developed. Increased demand will put pressure on an already scarce timber resource, and this could result in additional deforestation. An assessment is urgently needed to estimate future timber demands, available supply, and opportunities for national, regional and international procurement. Future wood supply should be obtained from sustainable sources and should take into account local wood preferences, climatic conditions and insect fauna. Possibilities for using alternative building materials, or reducing the amount of wood needed in building construction should also be investigated. UNEP's satellite assessment of remaining forests stands in Nuristan, Nangarhar and Kunar provinces has provided important new information on the level of deforestation in these areas. UNHCR is proposing to continue this analyses by studying opportunities for the procurement of Afghan timber to support the construction of 60,000 shelters. This study will provide additional information on existing national supplies, and the results could be used to form national timber procurement policies as well as to direct reforestation efforts.

In the medium to long term, the following policies and management activities will also be required:

94. Establish forest management legislation: Legislation should be developed to provide a framework for sustainable forest management. Such legislation should cover the regulation of timber and fuelwood harvesting, grazing and fire management, and dry land cultivation.

95. Undertake gradual implementation of export controls: High prices in Pakistan and abroad are exerting significant market pressure to harvest and export Afghan timber at unsustainable rates. Measures to reduce export levels by controls and taxation must be applied progressively to avoid violent confrontation. Incremental measures might include:

(a) Collection of data on volumes, revenues, and export routes for cross-border timber trade.

(b) Registration of the trade and imposition of low taxes.

(c) Channeling of all trade through a few border points, and closing down other illegal crossing points.

(d) Gradually increasing regulations and taxes so as to reduce export profits.

96. Institute grazing management and rotation systems: Rotational grazing schemes should be established to ensure that grazing pressure is lifted from a sequence of forest areas in order to achieve significant seedling survival. Assessments should be made to determine the carrying capacity of various forested lands for grazing, taking into account climatic variability and other ecological needs such as vegetation cover for soil stabilization, and forest regeneration.

97. Develop demonstration sites showing the viability and benefits of forest conservation: This should be done in areas where communities have decided to maintain forest cover for watershed protection and other purposes (such as in Shigal in Kunar province, and Darreh Nur in Nangarhar province). Clear comparisons should also be made with communities not engaging in forest conservation and protection in order to highlight the benefits. Communities which have demonstrated a commitment to sustainable forest management should be given further support and encouragement.

98. Promote strict protection of forest sites as components of a national protected areas system: None of the eastern conifer forest ecosystems are contained within existing protected areas. Options for the establishment of a single large protected area, several small nature reserves, and genetic reserves with buffer zones should be considered in order to protect biodiversity and retain examples of original land cover. All protection measures should be conducted with the cooperation and support of local communities.

■ Energy

Forests, air, water and other environmental goods are all affected by energy policies. The energy sector is already causing environmental problems throughout the energy supply chain, including pollution of the soil and water table emanating from oil and gas leakages, poor refinery and production processes, and air pollution from the combustion of fossil fuels. The situation may deteriorate further as future reconstruction places additional demands on limited energy supplies. Environmental considerations and costs must be taken into account in planning the revitalization of the energy sector. Recommendations for medium- and long-term actions by the Ministry of Water and Power, and other relevant stakeholders, are given below.

99. Increase the use of all renewable energy resources: The Afghan administration is currently focusing on developing renewable energy supplies exclusively from hydroelectric production. However, all possible sources of renewable energy should be considered, including wind, solar and biogas. The Ministry of Water and Power should establish targets and provide guidance in the development of the renewable energy sector. Benefits and assistance should be sought from the Clean-Development Mechanism of the Kyoto Protocol. Donors and international development assistance should be encouraged to support this growing technology area. Immediate studies should be undertaken to investigate the increased use of solar power for cooking and heating.

100. Use best available technologies when rebuilding the energy sector: In rebuilding central power and heating plants, national government, municipalities and industry should aim to reduce the use of inefficient and polluting household stoves and ovens. Donors and local and national authorities should promote the use of energy-production technologies that minimize environmental pollution.

101. Encourage small-scale hydroelectric development: Current plans envision major hydroelectric developments for power generation. However, the planning base is largely outdated, and does not take into account existing environmental conditions, needs and downstream users. The planning base needs to be updated and opportunities explored for the installation of small-scale hydropower plants in support of local community development. The lessons learned, findings and recommendations of the World Commission on Dams should also be considered to minimize social and environmental impacts, especially on downstream users.

102. Save and conserve energy: Energy savings can be made by improving the electricity distribution networks and efficiency of heating, lighting and cooking systems. The Afghan government should provide help to municipalities and industry in assessing energy-saving opportunities, setting incentives and giving guidance on energy-saving measures.

103. Assess the possibilities to construct combined heat and power plants: Combined heat and power (CHP) production could provide efficient and cost-effective heat and power solutions to many urban areas and industry. The government should set incentives and assist municipalities and industry in assessing CHP potential.

104. Manage community woodlots: People rely on forests and woodlands as an important source of fuel for heating and cooking. However, current fuelwood supplies are not being managed and will be completely exhausted if current trends continue. Focused efforts are urgently needed to manage existing forests and woodlands for sustainable use and to develop community woodlots to increase fuelwood supplies. Programmes are also needed to investigate and increase the efficiency of fuelwood burning.

■ Air Quality

In Afghanistan's urban areas, especially in Kabul, air quality is poor due to traffic emissions, pollution from individually heated houses and from dust. The combined effect of these emissions can generate serious risks to public health. Some of UNEP's results in the measurements of air quality were alarming. The Ministries of Public Health, Irrigation, Water Resources and Environment, and Mines and Industry will be key partners in addressing air quality issues. The following measures could be applied to address current conditions before they deteriorate any further.

105. Protect workers: The quality of air around industrial facilities applies equally within such sites, and is a major cause of problems with occupational health. In many cases, workers are being exposed on a daily basis to dangerous chemicals and are breathing polluted air. Many children, too, are working in such conditions. As a matter of urgency, health and environmental authorities should investigate working conditions in facilities where hazardous chemicals are used, and immediate action should be taken to protect workers, especially children, from unhealthy working conditions.

106. Improve public transport systems: All cities should assess mass transit measures that are being applied successfully in other parts of the world to fight traffic congestion and pollution. Numerous cities (such as Bogota, Columbia and Curitiba, Brazil) have successfully implemented rapid bus transit services, helping to alleviate air pollution levels while providing citizens with a timely and cost-effective mode of transport. In Kabul more advanced public transport systems need to be developed. A study should be undertaken on the feasibility of restoring the city's trolley-bus network. A precondition to this would be a stable electricity supply.

107. Use cleaner fuels: Poor-quality fossil fuels are contributing to the current air pollution problem. Quality standards and tax incentives should be established for fuel used in households for heating, as well as for diesel oil and gasoline used in the transport sector. Products with reduced emissions should carry lower overall taxes in order to increase their use. Introduction of better-quality, cleaner-burning fuels would help to diminish hydrocarbon concentrations and reduce health risks from air pollution.

108. Increase the use of natural gas: As demonstrated in India and Pakistan, natural gas can be used in both buses and small cars as an alternative to gasoline. This would improve air quality in city centres. As a first step, the government could set targets for natural gas use in public buses and taxis, and introduce incentives for conversion to natural gas.

109. Regularly inspect the transport sector: To improve traffic safety, regular inspection of cars, trucks and buses should be implemented and minimum operating conditions established. This should include regulation of air emissions.

110. Institute a central system of heating: Houses heated individually can be significant sources of pollution as the quality of fuel used is almost impossible to control. A central heating plant and distribution network in major towns like Kabul could help to reduce air pollution and increase energy efficiency.

111. Stop uncontrolled burning of wastes: Household wastes are burned in individual houses, inadequate incinerators or at waste collection sites or landfills. These practices are known to release a variety of toxic pollutants into the air, including cancer-causing dioxins and furans. The public should be alerted to the risks and uncontrolled burning of wastes should be stopped.

112. Manage industrial air pollution: As part of the environmental legislation, norms and standards should be introduced for the regulation and control of industrial air pollution. Economic incentives that promote the use of cleaner technologies for emissions control should also be developed.

■ Protected areas network and wildlife conservation

Protected areas have a number of important functions including conservation of species, genes and ecosystems, nature tourism, public education, recreation, and scientific study. Modern approaches to protected areas planning stress the need for community participation, and for multiple uses aimed to benefit residents as well as to maintain natural processes and ecological values. Evidence from around the world shows that with suitable design and management these twin goals can be achieved. In many instances, there is high potential for nature tourism as a complementary or alternative form of land use that can generate employment and income opportunities. The Ministry of Agriculture and Animal Husbandry, together with the Ministry of Irrigation, Water Resources and Environment and the Afghanistan Tourist Organization will be key partners in protected areas management. As Afghanistan develops a protected areas network, the following principles and activities should be considered.

113. Identify biodiversity hotspots and set protection targets: A comprehensive inventory is required of the existing ecosystems and wildlife in Afghanistan in order to identify areas with high biodiversity values, in particular those habitats and species most threatened. Some priority ecosystems can already be identified including conifer, pistachio, juniper and tugai forests, as well as the habitats of threatened species including snow leopard, Marco Polo sheep, markhor, urial, Bactrian deer, Asiatic black bear, Siberian cranes and white-headed ducks. Targets should be established for protecting a minimum percentage of the country based on the inventory and international best practice. While the 1987 World Commission on Environment and Development recommended protection targets of 12 per cent, many scientists now regard this as an arbitrary figure and recommend that actual targets should be set based on local conditions, threats and opportunities.

114. Introduce protected areas legislation: New protected areas legislation is required in order to provide a legal, institutional and management framework for a system of protected areas in Afghanistan. The legal status of Afghanistan's one national park, two wildlife reserves and three waterfowl sanctuaries also requires immediate clarification.

115. Establish protected areas as a managed resource: In keeping with a community-based approach, Afghanistan should establish the majority of its protected areas system to coincide with the principles of IUCN Category IV Managed Resource Protected Areas. Category IV areas are defined as "...containing predominantly unmodified natural systems, managed to ensure long-term protection and maintenance of biological diversity, while providing at the same time a sustainable flow of natural products and services to meet community needs".

116. Explore the feasibility of restoring degraded wetlands: All but one of the wetlands visited by UNEP were found to be compromised by a lack of water and no longer performing previous ecological roles, such as the provision of habitat for migrating or resident waterfowl. This condition has probably been caused by a combination of drought and excessive water extraction from upstream irrigation and deep wells. Feasibility studies should be undertaken to determine options for site rehabilitation. Technical assistance may be available through the Ramsar Convention's Montreux Record of wetlands at risk and small grants fund.

117. Monitor protected areas: ecological conditions and wildlife populations within managed resource protected areas should be carefully monitored to ensure human uses are within sustainable limits. Each area should have a manager and rangers to conduct basic monitoring.

118. Manage wildlife populations: Almost all the large mammal species in Afghanistan (including snow leopard, markhor, Marco Polo sheep and black bear) have been assessed as threatened with extinction. Tiger, cheetah and wild ass appear to have most likely disappeared from the country altogether. Afghanistan is centrally located along major flyways for migratory birds, several species of which are classified as critically endangered such as the

Siberian crane and white-headed duck. Wildlife and natural habitats within Afghanistan are therefore of international, as well as national importance, and the country has an opportunity to play an important role in maintaining global biodiversity. The opportunity also exists to obtain direct benefits from wildlife conservation through job creation and ecotourism. Useful measures would include:

(a) Develop appropriate legislation for wildlife management, protection and enforcement with a particular emphasis on threatened species. Depleted populations of wildlife need to be allowed to recover. Hunting pressure can be relieved through appropriate incentive measures aimed at ensuring long-term sustainability.

(b) Create community and curriculum conservation education initiatives which focus on the importance of wildlife to both ecosystem function and cultural heritage.

(c) Survey and monitor populations of all wildlife. Create baseline data that can be used to generate management plans to ensure the continuing survival of wild species, especially endemic and threatened species. Use data from surveys to identify key habitats of endemic and threatened species and biodiversity hotspots, and use this information to inform the development of the protected areas network, including buffer zones and a series of wildlife corridors connecting protected areas if necessary.

(d) Implement the provisions of the Convention on International Trade in Endangered Species (CITES) and the Convention on Biological Diversity. Consider the benefits to wildlife that could be obtained by ratifying the Ramsar Convention on Wetlands and the Convention on the Conservation of Migratory Species (CMS).

(e) Educate international aid workers and security forces about illegal trade and hunting of endangered species, and discourage purchasing furs or parts of endangered animals.

119. Develop transboundary protected areas: Some of the most important biodiversity sites in Afghanistan, such as the Wakhan Corridor, Sistan wetlands and the provinces of Kunar and Nuristan occur along the border with other countries. Opportunities for establishing transboundary protected areas should be investigated, including options for linking smaller protected areas with transboundary wildlife corridors.

120. Protect green spaces, green belts and trees in urban areas: Residents in Kabul, Herat, Jalalabad and other cities in Afghanistan have identified the need to continue to protect green spaces and plant trees throughout the urban network. Such areas not only provide people with an escape from the realities of urban life, but also increase habitat for birds and other small animals, provide areas for children to play, experience and learn about nature, and provide local communities with opportunities for self-taught and professionally led environmental education. All urban areas should continue efforts to protect remaining green space, and plant additional vegetation. This is an important priority given current population increases and pressures for urban expansion. Particular attention should be paid to Kole Hashmat Khan, given its multiple use potential. Cities vulnerable to sand dune movements should also re-establish forest belts on city margins in order to act as a natural barrier to sand.

121. Promote tourism development: Afghanistan's protected areas network could become an important attraction for national and international tourism. Opportunities for developing eco-tourism in protected areas should be explored.

6

■ Desertification

Afghanistan is highly susceptible to desertification, a process of land degradation in arid, semi-arid and dry sub-humid areas that results in reduced biological communities and productivity, whether caused by climatic variations or human or other activities. Afghanistan's rangelands are at particular risk of desertification. In these areas, widespread grazing has reduced vegetation cover and is exposing soils to erosion. Many communities have had to reduce or dispose of livestock because of reduced quality of rangelands. Other factors influencing the spread of desertification are deforestation and uncontrolled extraction of water resources. A broad and sustained effort will need to be undertaken by the Ministries of Irrigation, Water Resources and Environment, Rural Development, and Agriculture and Animal Husbandry in order to address the challenge of desertification. The following measures should be undertaken immediately:

122. Stabilize sand dunes and soils: To prevent sand dune movement and soil erosion, immediate measures should be taken to plant stabilizing vegetation. Traditional techniques and labour-intensive approaches should be adopted when possible.

123. Reseed highly degraded rangeland: Labour-intensive programmes to reseed and or replant degraded rangelands should be developed.

124. Reduce grazing and dry land cultivation in vulnerable areas: Immediate measures should be undertaken to develop incentive or compensation schemes to reduce grazing pressures and dry land cultivation in vulnerable areas. At the same time, opportunities to enhance other agricultural production, for example, by making improvements to irrigation supply or rangeland condition should be investigated.

125. Map areas vulnerable to desertification: A countrywide assessment should be conducted to identify and classify areas that are currently experiencing or are vulnerable to desertification. This would include identifying soils prone to erosion as well as areas vulnerable to drought. This assessment should be linked directly to land-use planning and restoration strategies.

126. Create community-based rangeland assessment and management plans: Develop regular monitoring of rangeland condition and determine sustainable stocking densities for rangeland areas taking into account natural climatic variation. Work with local communities to develop grazing regimes that optimize benefits and range condition. Strong consideration should be given to management systems that achieve significant survival of vegetation cover from year to year, for example rotational grazing plots.

127. Establish representative rangeland areas where grazing is excluded or experimentally controlled: This can be done as part of the national protected areas system, providing a reserve of rangeland species and, through experimental control plots, helping to establish optimum stocking levels.

■ Plant resources for food and agriculture

Pistachio, almond, walnut, and apricot are among the fruit and nut trees that provide important food resources and valuable export commodities. Afghanistan holds a wide range of wild species, domestic varieties and wild relatives of domestic forms. The following measures should be undertaken by the Ministry of Agriculture and Animal Husbandry to protect this important resource.

Post-Conflict Environmental Assessment

128. Re-establish gene banks: Extend existing initiatives to collect, document and store seedbanks of fruit and nut trees, both to maintain genetic diversity and to multiply sapling stocks and increase planting of fruit and nut trees.

129. Promote community-based orchards: Investigate improved marketing systems to support and enhance locally owned orchards and maintain their income.

130. Promote local varieties of cereal: During the rehabilitation of the agricultural sector, preference should be given to local varieties of cereal that are typically suited to local combinations of topography and climate.

131. Promote sustainable agriculture practices: During the rehabilitation of the agricultural sector, opportunities to develop sustainable agricultural practices covering economic, social and environmental considerations should be investigated. Measures to support sustainable farming practices should be linked with efforts to maintain landscapes, habitats of high biodiversity value, and biosafety standards. Certification procedures could be developed to ensure that basic standards are met and that the origin of all products is traceable. This would help to build consumer confidence and awareness, and improve marketing potential for export.

■ International environmental conventions

Multilateral environmental agreements (MEAs) cover a broad range of subjects addressing global environmental problems. As Afghanistan reconnects with the international community, it needs to implement existing international commitments and consider the potential benefits of joining other agreements. However, to benefit from MEAs Afghanistan will need to make important changes and build capacities in these areas.

132. Strengthen the focal point for MEAs: The Ministry of Foreign Affairs has political responsibility for MEAs. Immediate measures should be taken to strengthen and improve its capacity for coordinating information, policies and decisions with the sectoral ministries that have responsibilities for technical matters and field implementation. Coordination mechanisms between foreign and national policy on MEA should also be developed to ensure a harmonized approach.

133. Prioritize international environmental conventions: A step-wise approach should be taken to the ratification of new agreements based on needs, benefits and obligations. Ratification priorities should be clearly identified by sector ministries and communicated to the Ministry of Foreign Affairs. Afghanistan should also aim for consolidated and simplified reporting in renewing its commitment to international agreements.

134. Activate and implement existing agreements: Afghanistan is currently a party to five environmental conventions. Immediate steps should be taken to activate existing agreements and begin to obtain technical assistance and financial benefits:

(a) **International Convention to Combat Desertification (CCD):** Although a party to the CCD since 1995, a treaty which aims to develop collaborative action to reduce or reverse desertification in susceptible countries worldwide, civil disorder and armed conflict since then have limited the country's participation. The CCD could provide important technical support and funding from the Global Environment Facility (GEF) for addressing land degradation. To reactivate participate in the CCD the following actions are required: (i) designate a national focal point, notify the CCD secretariat, and clarify membership fees; (ii) conduct a national awareness-raising seminar and develop a national report on current conditions, needs, strategies and available resources; (iii) formulate a national action plan which outlines a strategy to address desertification and defines needs for international assistance; (iv) develop project proposals for submission to GEF for funding, such as national mapping of vulnerable and degraded areas, and establishing priority areas for rehabilitation.

(b) **Convention on Biological Diversity (CBD):** Afghanistan only recently ratified the CBD and has taken no significant steps towards implementation. The CBD could assist Afghanistan in the sustainable use of its resource base, in the development of a protected areas network, and in the equitable sharing of benefits arising from genetic resources. To benefit from this convention, the following steps should be taken: (i) designate a national focal point, notify the CBD secretariat, and clarify membership fees; (ii) select an implementing agency and formulate a national biodiversity strategy and action plan; (iii) develop project proposals for submission to GEF for funding, such as conducting an inventory of national biodiversity, and identifying biodiversity 'hot spots', and developing a protected area network and relevant management plans. In addition, Afghanistan should consider ratifying the Cartagena Protocol on Biosafety in order to protect biological diversity from the potential risks posed by living modified organisms resulting from modern biotechnology. The Biosafety Protocol ensures that countries are provided with the information necessary to make informed decisions before agreeing to the import of such organisms into their territory.

(c) **Basel Convention on the Control of Transboundary Movements of Hazardous Wastes and their Disposal:** Afghanistan signed this convention in 1989 but did not ratify. The convention would assist Afghanistan in controlling the transboundary movement of hazardous waste, minimizing domestic production of such waste, and preventing its illegal dumping. Afghanistan should strongly consider ratifying this convention so that future industrial activities can obtain access to technical assistance in hazardous waste management.

(d) **International Convention for the Protection of the World Cultural and Natural Heritage:** Afghanistan became a member in 1979. The convention lists natural and culture World Heritage Sites and obliges parties to fulfill certain management responsibilities. At present only a single cultural site, the Minaret and archaeological remains of Jam, are listed. Both Band-e-Amir and Pamir-i-Buzurg should qualify as natural heritage sites under the convention, and serious consideration should be given to listing these sites. This would increase international recognition and tourism opportunities, and promote improved management. Afghanistan should also undertake an analysis of additional natural and cultural sites that could be listed.

(e) **Convention on International Trade in Endangered Species of Wild Flora and Fauna (CITES):** Afghanistan became a member of CITES in 1985 and steps are now being taken to implement the convention. The Department of Forests and Range in the Ministry of Agriculture has been designated as the management authority to administer a licensing system. Recommended steps to further implement this convention include: (i) designate a scientific authority with the capacity to study the effects of trade on various listed species; (ii) train customs officials in the detection of species listed under CITES; (iii) develop mechanisms to track import and export of listed species, as well as licensing systems; (iv) conduct periodic reporting to the CITES secretariat. Assistance should also be requested from the CITES secretariat to develop awareness programmes for international aid workers and security forces to discourage the purchase of furs or parts of endangered animals.

(f) **United Nations Framework Convention on Climate Change (UNFCCC):** Afghanistan, which ratified the convention in 2002, is vulnerable to global climate change through desertification and drought. International assistance will be needed to mitigate or adapt to such impacts. In order to benefit from the convention, and the Kyoto Protocol, the following steps should be taken: (i) designate a national focal point, notify the UNFCCC secretariat, and clarify membership fees; (ii) request assistance from the LDC Expert Group on developing a national adaptation programme of action; (iii) communicate voluntary participation in the Clean Development Mechanism (CDM), establish a CDM focal point and inter-ministry coordination mechanism, and establish a process for reviewing CDM proposals against national development priorities; (iv) develop project proposals for submission to GEF for funding, such as climate monitoring and mapping areas vulnerable to drought and flooding from Glacial Lake Outburst Flood (GLOF) events.

(g) **Develop CDM projects:** To obtain immediate benefits from the CDM, the government should encourage the development of small-scale projects, in collaboration with NGOs and private companies, and implement them as unilateral CDM projects. Such projects could include energy production from biomass, or the capture of solar energy for cooking and heating. The certified emission reductions units (CERs) resulting from these small projects could then be offered to international CER purchasers. The development and implementation of larger projects in the energy, infrastructure and industry sectors should be developed in cooperation with donor agencies and international investors. The Afghan government should signal the willingness to implement all potential projects under the CDM. The CDM possibilities should be evaluated for each project individually, in parallel with the respective project development activities. Screening potential CDM opportunities could be integrated into the EIA process.

(h) **Convention on Wetlands of International Importance (Ramsar):** Once considered to have at least three wetlands of international importance for waterfowl, Afghanistan is not, however, a party to the convention. All three of these wetlands were observed by UNEP to be completely dry in 2002. In the event of natural recovery or rehabilitation, Afghanistan should seek international support to achieve more effective management of wetlands for local community benefit and for wetland species and multiple ecosystem functions and services. The identification of sites meeting Ramsar criteria would enhance the possibility of obtaining GEF funding under the Convention on Biodiversity, since wetlands are important reservoirs of biodiversity.

(i) **Convention on the Protection and the Use of Transboundary Watercourses and International Lakes:** This convention was established for the member states of the Economic Commission for Europe (ECE) to strengthen measures for the management of transboundary surface and ground waters. A memorandum of understanding or similar could be established for Afghanistan to participate or have observer status in ongoing discussions on the water resources of the Amu Darya basin.

(j) **Convention on the Conservation of Migratory Species (CMS):** Afghanistan has numerous mammals, including Marco Polo sheep, that could benefit from this convention. However, the country does not need to become a member in order to join one of its associated agreements. The CMS secretariat has prepared, or is in the process of preparing, a number of agreements, covering the Siberian crane, houbara bustard and snow leopard, from which Afghanistan could benefit. Coordinated action for the recognition of the Central-South Asian migratory waterbird flyway, involving the protection of stopover habitats, is also in process.

Site-specific recommendations

Many of the following site-specific recommendations will require immediate action by site owners and responsible authorities in order to protect human health and prevent further environmental degradation. Technical assistance will also be required from the international community. However, long-term solutions to prevent such chronic environmental problems will require new legislation to be developed jointly between the Ministry of Irrigation, Water Resources and Environment and the relevant sector ministries. In most cases, implementation will be at the municipal level in cooperation with the relevant industrial sites, public facilities and other stakeholders.

■ Waste management:

135. Herat:

(a) Determine the risk of floodwater at the Qamar Qalla landfill site and assess options for risk reduction, including closing down the site.

(b) Reduce the amount of soil being transported to the site. This could be done at a transfer station nearer the city, where the soil and inert particles (sand, soil, stone dust, etc.) can be screened out of the waste matrix. Alternatively, a screen could be installed at the waste disposal site to extract soils from the waste mass. The latter alternative is less favourable because it contributes to the waste of fuel and extra vehicle use.

(c) Divide the dumpsite into sections and use a tipping-plan. The waste in non-active parts of the dumpsite should be covered with soil to reduce the risk of spreading diseases by flies, insects and wind-blown waste. This would also reduce risks to the people who are recycling materials from the site.

(d) Leachate and gas management needs to be considered. Increased waste production, more diverse waste products and the prospect of future precipitation make this an important issue.

(e) Environmental Impact Assessments (EIA) should be applied to each potential future waste disposal site. Sites should be ranked prior to selection. The selection process should take account of geology, hydrology and groundwater sources in order to ascertain any likely environmental problems. Capacity-building measures should run in parallel to the EIA process in order to facilitate an understanding of municipal waste management methods.

136. Kabul:

(a) A holistic waste management strategy is needed for Kabul if the city is to develop and meet anticipated waste management resource requirements in the coming decade. Districts where residences face extreme health risks, such as Districts 5 and 6, should be prioritized for waste collection and management in order to reduce risks to human health.

(b) The size of Kabul justifies a fully mechanized waste transfer station that could bale the waste and separate inert material from the waste. A proper municipal refuse facility would lead to greater efficiency, higher recycling levels and better use of vehicles and fuel resources. It would also facilitate better management practice at the landfill site, where waste could be placed in bales. This would optimize space and minimize leachate and gas production.

(c) Groundwater should be protected from the dumpsite with a clay lining or layer of geo-textile. This is especially important because of the dumpsite's close proximity to one of Kabul's main drinking water well fields and strategically important groundwater resources.

(d) The burning of waste at the dumpsite must be controlled. Consumption is expected to increase in the future, and with it the ratio of combustible materials (such as paper or plastics) will undoubtedly increase. It will be important to prevent emission of hazardous substances (such as dioxin from plastics) that are given off by burning waste.

(e) It is essential that the municipality develop a remediation/restoration strategy for the now inactive Cham-Tala site. This should include profiling of the site and covering it with soil to prevent the washing out of contaminants by precipitation.

(f) Capacity building, including training programmes, should be offered at all levels throughout the public sector to ensure that the municipality adopts techniques and best practice from appropriate countries.

137. Kandahar:

(a) The municipality should develop a waste action plan in order to determine the vehicles and equipment needed, and site remediation options, where appropriate.

(b) Using environmental risk assessment, the municipality should identify a site on the outskirts of the city for a waste transfer station where wastes can be sorted, segregated and baled. Taking the same approach, the municipality should then identify an appropriate disposal site for the baled waste.

(c) Introduce safe processes for handling and disposing of medical and slaughterhouse waste. High-temperature incineration or gasification is the preferred option.

138. Mazar-e-Sharif:

(a) Waste should be screened to separate soil from organic matter, which could possibly be mixed into compost. Debris, plastics, paper and so on could be baled.

(b) Continue to promote recycling and waste awareness in cooperation with UN-Habitat or other partners, as needed.

(c) The municipality should address the issue of the redundant quarry adjacent to the present waste disposal site and incorporate the site into any new plans.

■ Wastewater:

139. Herat:

(a) As a first step, the existing outlet from the wastewater pipeline should be extended to reach the low-water level in the Carobar River.

(b) It is imperative that a wastewater treatment plant be installed before, or in parallel with, any further extension of the sewer pipeline, because additional sewer pipe work will result in a higher volume of untreated wastewater being discharged into an already stressed river system. Any wastewater treatment facility should be fenced to prevent public access.

(c) Slurry from septic tanks should be treated at the wastewater facility. The application of untreated sewage to agricultural land is a high-risk activity and can lead to the entry of *E. Coli* and bacteriological coliform into the food chain and/or groundwater.

140. **Kabul:**

(a) All districts require an urgent further assessment of wastewater infrastructure and possible sources of cross-contamination of drinking water supplies. Wastewater and water supply officials will need to coordinate information and activities.

(b) In the context of a broader wastewater agenda for Kabul, the feasibility of wastewater treatment for all districts should be thoroughly assessed.

(c) The existing wastewater facility for Districts 9 and 16 should be assessed to ensure that it is operating to best available practice in terms of the process being used. The plant's treatment technologies (including oxygenation/flocculation) should be upgraded. The municipality should be assisted in procuring the necessary process chemicals that are now unavailable.

(d) An assessment should be made of the viability of extending the wastewater collection system for Districts 9 and 16 to other districts and the impact this would have on the operation and size of the present plant.

(e) Disposal of the plant's sludge onto land should be suspended until the plant can upgrade its treatment technology (oxygenation/flocculation) and obtain the chemicals necessary to the process. Sludge composition should be regularly monitored to ensure safety levels are maintained.

■ Water supply:

141. **Herat:**

(a) There is a considerable need to extend the water supply network, which at present only reaches about 30 per cent of the city's population. As a first step, carry out an investigation of groundwater resources in order to identify water of sufficient quality and quantity. Following this, there will be a need to extend the well fields and water supply pipelines. Such an initiative should be coordinated with a groundwater management programme.

(b) It is crucial that proper sanitary protection zones are established around the deep wells to ensure a safe water supply in the long term.

(c) Although Herat has portable water-testing equipment, additional equipment is needed to cover the city's needs.

142. **Kabul:**

(a) There is an urgent need to create protection zones around all of Kabul's well fields.

(b) Carry out a study to examine the risk that the Kampanie dumpsite poses to the nearby groundwater resources. The study should also identify alternative resources for the city's future water supply.

(c) Extend the coverage of Kabul's water supply network. This will require a hydrogeological investigation to identify additional water resources of sufficient quality and quantity. Several new deep wells, in addition to those planned by

Kreditanstalt für Wiederaufbau (KfW), will need to be drilled. Substantial distances of new pipeline and many additional public or private taps will also be needed. It would be best to initiate this process with a feasibility study that can establish precise needs, quantify costs, and take into account the ongoing efforts in this area, particular KfW's work.

143. Kandahar:

(a) The municipality should identify safe, alternative groundwater resources in the region for future exploitation. Additional resources would enable the city to expand coverage of its drinking water supply to a larger percentage of its population, the vast majority of whom are currently supplied by shallow groundwater of questionable quality.

144. Mazar-e-Sharif:

(a) There is a considerable need to extend the city's supply network, which reaches less than half of the population. A World Bank project is expected to reconstruct and rehabilitate the existing network only. Extending the network will require identifying groundwater resources of proper quality and quantity. Such an initiative should be closely coordinated with a groundwater management programme.

(b) Sanitary protection zones are urgently needed around the city's deep wells. In addition, monitoring wells are needed at the well fields to assess pollution risk and ensure a safe water supply in the long term.

■ Hospitals

145. Herat Regional Hospital:

(a) It is absolutely essential that staff begin to manage clinical waste with appropriate waste containers and protective clothing. Better awareness and best practice procedures should be introduced through training programmes for all hospital management and staff.

(b) The existing, wholly inadequate incinerator should be replaced by a new, more appropriate low-cost unit as soon as possible. The content of the waste being burned needs to be managed so that dioxin, furan and heavy metal emissions are not released into the atmosphere. The area around the incinerator should be fenced immediately to prevent unauthorized access to the site and to protect the public from the risks associated with medical waste.

(c) The water supply system needs to be significantly improved. Groundwater management is needed for the entire area, and the wells need protective buffer zones. A chlorine purification system should be installed. The water pipeline network should be rehabilitated to repair leaks. All pipeline connection pits should be covered to prevent contamination by dumped waste. The pressure in the pipeline system should maintained 24 hours a day to prevent infiltration of contaminated water.

(d) In the longer term, the existing deep drinking water well should be closed and a new water resource identified. In addition to being contaminated with *E. coli* and total coliforms, the well is too close to the underground oil storage tank. The risk of cross-contamination is likely to increase when the drought ceases, the groundwater table rises, and contaminants are washed out.

(e) The two underground oil tanks should be checked for leakage and repaired, as necessary. Serious consideration should also be given to moving the tanks above ground. The tanks' filling procedures should also be improved to prevent further spills.

(f) The stored oil barrels and activities related to them should occur within a closed container. Proper oil management requires second containment units involving 'spill trays' that collect leaking or spilled oil.

(g) The fuel pipe system in the generator station should be checked for leaks and repaired as necessary. Staff at the station should have access to oil-absorbing granulate in case of accidents.

(h) The wastewater treatment and storage systems should be thoroughly assessed.

146. Mazar-e-Sharif Civil Hospital:

(a) In view of its severely deteriorated infrastructure and poor environmental conditions, the hospital's continued viability should be examined. Should its continued operation be deemed essential, investments should be made to improve the facility and its environmental practices as quickly as possible.

(b) Medical waste should be segregated and properly disposed of onsite according to best practices in health care waste management. It is absolutely essential that staff manage clinical waste with protective clothing. Better awareness and best practice procedures should be introduced urgently through training programmes for all hospital management and staff.

(c) The water supply system needs to be improved significantly, and management of groundwater is needed for the entire area. The hand pump needs a protective buffer zone. A chlorine purification system should be installed, and the water pipeline network should be rehabilitated to repair leaks.

(d) The practice of dumping waste into the former 15-m well pit should cease immediately to prevent further potential contamination of groundwater, and the waste in the well should be cleaned out.

(e) The condition of the septic tanks should be examined immediately to determine the extent of soil and groundwater contamination in the area.

(f) New wastewater treatment facilities should be provided.

147. Mirwais Civilian Hospital:

(a) Awareness of proper clinical waste management practices is urgently needed. Better awareness and best practice procedures should be introduced through training programmes for all hospital management and staff. It is absolutely essential that staff manage clinical waste with protective clothing.

(b) The waste management system, including the onsite dump, the International Committee of the Red Cross (ICRC) dumpsite and the underground syringe storage area, should be assessed thoroughly. At a minimum, the hospital needs improved waste management infrastructure and equipment, accompanied by training in the development of a best practice waste management and infection control plan.

(c) The incinerator should be loaded mechanically, and care taken to minimize emissions of heavy metals, dioxin and furans from, for example, the burning of plastic waste.

(d) The application of hospital sludge to land should be suspended, and the sludge evaluated, particularly in terms of its suitability for onsite drying and burning.

■ Industrial sites

148. Shiburghan Oil Refineries:

(a) From an environmental point of view, the only sustainable solution is to close down the site. In the short term, the site should be thoroughly investigated, an EIA performed, and an action plan developed to reduce immediately the loads of air, soil and water pollution being produced. Special emphasis should be placed on the oil-handling procedures being used.

(b) Groundwater in the vicinity of the refineries should be monitored.

(c) The refineries' sludge should be disposed of safely. If it must be burned, it should only be done in a controlled environment that will prevent additional deterioration of air quality.

149. Mawlawy Oil Storage Facility:

(a) The handling procedures for the two oil storage areas need to be vastly improved to minimize oil spills and leaks. A thorough programme of leakage detection is needed for the tanks and the pipeline systems. Leaking storage tanks and pipelines should be repaired immediately or taken out of use.

(b) Several monitoring wells should be installed downstream from the oil storage facilities in order to evaluate potential migration of oil products into groundwater.

(c) Monitoring of all drinking water wells in a 1 km radius downstream of the site should be carried out immediately in order to identify and address any problems arising from dissolved hydrocarbons in the groundwater. This should be combined with regular monitoring of drinking water quality.

(d) Gas monitoring wells should be drilled and proper monitoring equipment should be installed.

150. Sar-e-Pol Crude Oil Terminal:

(a) The oil tanks and the pipeline system should be checked immediately for potential leakage, and proper management procedures carried out to prevent future spills.

(b) To prevent spilled oil from infiltrating soil and groundwater, concrete plates should be placed under the oil tanks and loading facilities. The plates should drain oil to a concrete collection basin and an oil separator, allowing spilled oil to be recycled.

(c) If feasible, the onsite refinery should be renovated. This would eliminate the need for crude oil to be transported to the environmentally hazardous private refineries in Shiburghan. An alternative would be to decommission the site, carry out an environmental assessment and clean-up any contamination.

(d) Remediation of the groundwater does not appear necessary at this time, however a more detailed site visit should be undertaken to verify this determination. Monitoring of water wells downstream of the oil refinery would enable the presence and level of free-phase oil products and dissolved hydrocarbons in the groundwater to be detected.

151. Zhora Plastic Recycling/Shoe Factory:

(a) An immediate audit of the health conditions and environmental impact of this and similar facilities should be made. Ideally, such infrastructures should be relocated away from residential areas, in commercial zones. Measures should be taken to manage the use of process chemicals properly and to minimize contamination of air, soil and groundwater.

(b) Unless these kinds of companies are required to adopt a far more health and safety conscious working environment, consideration should be given to closing them down.

(c) The workforce should be provided immediately with proper protective equipment, and the rooms should be ventilated. The length of worker exposure should be limited and should not under any circumstances continue 24 hours per day. In the longer term, management and staff should be trained in basic environmental management systems.

(d) The issue of the Zhora Factory should be addressed as a matter of urgency as children are being exposed to serious health risks. Protection of children should be of the highest priority as they are a vulnerable group without the ability to demand better conditions. It is unacceptable by any measure for children to be working and sleeping in such a toxic environment.

152. Brick Factory:

(a) The entire brick-making industry should be assessed from the perspective of air emissions. Particular emphasis should be placed on determining whether a cleaner burning fuel (such as natural gas) could be used in the process.

(b) To the extent possible, brick production facilities should be moved away from urban areas. This would protect residential air quality and reduce the negative health effects of smoke emissions. In the longer term, the industry should be guided toward cleaner production methods.

(c) The capacity of local authorities to monitor and regulate air emissions needs to be strengthened.

153. Zuri Battery Company:

(a) The plant should install a gas scrubber for the lead smelter in order to minimize air polluting emissions.

(b) There should be a strict requirement for workers to wear protective clothing and facemasks to prevent inhalation of lead-contaminated dust. Workers should also receive information on the risks confronting them in the work environment.

(c) An air ventilation system should be installed in the battery charging room and the work floor in the battery recycling area should be cleaned regularly.

(d) With international financial support and sharing of best practice, this well-run facility could expand its operation to recycle plastic and oxide.

154. Asphalt Factory:

(a) The plant's management and entire daily operations should be reviewed. Much can and should be done to improve working conditions and safety.

(b) There is a need to reduce or eliminate heavy oil spillages from leaking pipelines, and to improve oil storage and handling, especially during the delivery process.

(c) To prevent spilled oil from infiltrating soil and groundwater, concrete plates should be placed under the oil tanks and loading facilities. The plates should drain oil to a concrete collection basin and an oil separator, allowing spilled oil to be recycled.

(d) The plant should install improved technology that would reduce air emissions and reduce the health and environmental risks to local residents.

■ Protected areas

155. Band-e-Amir:

(a) The government should re-establish and manage Band-e-Amir as a national park.

(b) The clearance of mines around the area should be made a priority to ensure the safety of visitors and local people.

(c) The government should issue an interim directive to all government and military personnel indicating that hunting by government staff is banned within a 10-km radius of Band-e-Amir and that fishing with explosives is not permitted.

(d) At the earliest opportunity, a management and land-use planning process should be undertaken in close consultation with local people and relevant government agencies. The resultant plan should ensure that all people living around Band-e-Amir, including the people of Kupruk, benefit from national park status and tourism development. Procedures for ensuring continuing local input into park management should be established. The management plan should also outline ways to reduce or control various pressures, including vehicle use within the park, excess harvesting of vegetation, litter, extension of irrigation networks, dry land farming, hunting and fishing. Tourism activities, including minimum standards for tourist facilities and opportunities for cost recovery for park management, should be developed immediately.

(e) Undertake an analysis leading to the possible nomination of Band-e-Amir as a UNESCO World Heritage Natural Site. Nominating Band-e-Amir would obligate the government to develop a management plan and institute effective legal protection. It would also help to increase international awareness of the site.

156. Wakhan Corridor and Pamir-i-Buzurg:

(a) The Pamir-i-Buzurg Wildlife Reserve should be maintained as a protected area in accordance with IUCN's Level IV protected area category. The legal status of this reserve should be clarified immediately, and a management plan adopted. To support this plan, detailed ecological studies should be conducted to survey wildlife populations, understand the forage relations between livestock and the Marco Polo sheep, assess the extent of pasture degradation, understand human-wildlife interactions, and evaluate the extent of potential disease transfers between domestic and wild herbivores.

(b) The entire Wakhan Corridor is a biodiversity 'hotspot', containing populations of a variety of threatened species including snow leopard, ibex and Marco polo sheep. It is essential, considering the mobility of human and wildlife populations, and the traditional trading links through the Wakhan, for community-based planning to take a holistic approach to the needs of the region. Given its unique status and condition, the entire area should be managed as a conservation unit. All management activities should be aimed at conserving its considerable landscape and wildlife values, while at the same time meeting the needs and aspirations of local people and developing income opportunities, including from tourism. As a first step, a feasibility study should be conducted to determine how the entire Wakhan Corridor could be managed as a protected area, and how opportunities for tourism could be maximized and benefits shared with local communities. Mechanisms to compensate farmers for loss of livestock from wildlife must also be assessed.

(c) Undertake an analysis leading to the possible nomination of either the Pamir-i-Buzurg Wildlife Reserve or the entire Wakhan Corridor as a UNESCO World Heritage Natural Site.

(d) Although the political obstacles are daunting, management activities for the Wakhan should be informed by a vision in which all the countries bordering the Wakhan come together to establish an international 'Peace Park'. As a first step, the boundaries of existing or proposed protected areas in neighbouring countries should be identified. Support for a transboundary protected area among local communities as well as governments should also be assessed.

157. Sistan basin:

(a) The wetlands of the Sistan basin, including the lakes of Hamoun-i-Puzak, Hamoun-e-Sabari, and Hamoun-e-Helmand were critical for migrating and resident waterfowl. A comprehensive ecological rehabilitation of the wetlands should be undertaken in order to restore the area to its previous condition. As a first step, the amount of water required to recharge at least one of the lakes e.g. Lake Hamoun-i-Puzak should be determined. If the amount can be met by a small but consistent release from the Kajaki dam, then serious consideration should be given to releasing the water. This decision will require both community support and transboundary cooperation from Iran. If the decision is taken to restore the wetlands, international assistance should be sought from the Ramsar Convention.

(b) Following successful restoration of the wetlands, they should be designated and managed as a transboundary protected area, with joint management by Iran and Afghanistan. The wetlands should also be recognized as an internally important site for migratory waterfowl and added to the Ramsar list.

158. Ab-e-Estada:

(a) Undertake a systematic hydrological study of the main watersheds around Ab-e-Estada (Gardez, Ghazni, and Nahara) emphasizing offtakes from dams, direct irrigation diversions, water pumps, and evaporation. The study should recommend optimal water allocation strategies that maximize sustainable benefits to all stakeholders.

(b) Launch a conservation education strategy to raise awareness among local community members about the importance of the lake to the ecological, economic and climatic well-being of the area.

(c) If ecological conditions and local sentiments allow, initiate a management planning process leading to legislative and *de facto* protection of the water and wildlife resources through cooperative management by government and local communities. Such a plan should ensure supply of sufficient water to the lake to maintain ecological values.

(d) A study of falcon-trapping at Ab-e-Estada should be carried out to gather information necessary to develop regulations that ensure the long-term viability of the activity.

(e) If Afghanistan becomes a party to the Ramsar Conservation, consideration should be given to listing this site.

159. Dasht-e-Nawar:

(a) The hydrology of Dasht-e-Nawar should be studied to provide data necessary for the development of a water allocation strategy that ensures the ecological integrity of the lake and the surrounding basin. In particular, the significance of the springs on the west side of the lake should be examined to better understand their biodiversity and ecological significance.

(b) In consultation with local people, a management plan should be developed for Dasht-e-Nawar that addresses the issues of water allocation, land-use planning, and protection measures. A resource inventory, including a biodiversity survey, should also be conducted and appropriate ecological boundaries established for the protected area.

(c) If Afghanistan becomes a party to the Ramsar Conservation, consideration should be given to listing this site.

(d) Develop an environmental education programme to create awareness amongst the people around Dasht-e-Nawar of the need to conserve natural resources for the benefit of the area's ecology and economy and to maintain traditional cultural values.

160. Kole Hashmat Khan:

(a) Kole Hashmat Khan should be protected as an important waterfowl staging and breeding area and as an urban 'green area'.

(b) Undertake a hydrological analysis of Kole Hashmat Khan to establish the level of water available in the Logar River system, and the offtakes of water through evaporation, irrigation channels and wells.

(c) A water management plan for the Logar River system should be developed, addressing water priorities and allocations.

(d) The ditch built around Kole Hashmat Khan should be filled and, other options should be considered for controlling access to the wetland.

(e) The Afghan government should formally establish ownership of Kole Hashmat Khan and the surrounding lands.

(f) Facilities should be built to house the present game guards.

(g) A management plan should be developed to protect the wetland from urban encroachment and unsustainable uses. Educational and recreational facilities should also be established to enable local communities to recognize the importance and benefits of the wetland system and derive benefits from the lake area.

161. Imam Sahib and Darqad:

(a) A detailed ecological survey should be conducted of both Imam Sahib and Darqad to determine existing plant and animal species, and to investigate community interest in designating them as protected areas.

(b) Opportunities should be investigated for assisting internally displaced people currently living on the forested islands and resettling them on the mainland.

162. Ajar Valley:

(a) Invite trusted and influential third parties to mediate a negotiated settlement of hostilities in Khamard.

(b) Once the political situation is normalized, undertake an on-the-ground assessment of wildlife populations and rangeland conditions, impacts of farmland expansion and grazing, and community organization and support for environmental protection.

(c) If protection measures are considered to be politically, socially and biologically feasible, develop a management plan in consultation with local inhabitants.

(d) Seek to engage the interest of the former Afghan King as a means of providing the Ajar Valley Wildlife Reserve with historical continuity, local support, and broader credibility.

163. Nuristan and Kunar:

(a) The provinces of Nuristan and Kunar may well contain the best-preserved stands of conifer forest in Afghanistan, as well as healthy populations of wildlife. However, none of these stands are currently incorporated in the protected areas network. Serious consideration should be given to the establishment of a single large protected area, or several small nature and genetic reserves, that would not be logged, and buffer zones where lower-level impacts would be allowed. A study should be conducted to determine areas of high biodiversity. In addition, mechanisms to pay communities for lost revenues by not logging key areas should be investigated.

ANNEXES

A. Clean Development Mechanism and Afghanistan

B. Laboratory analyses and sample results

C. Additional field mission photos

D. Literature cited

E. List of contributors

Annex A

Clean Development Mechanism and Afghanistan

The United Nations Framework Convention on Climate Change (UNFCCC), which entered into force in 1994, established an international legal framework to address global climate change. Parties to the convention agreed to stabilize greenhouse gas (GHG) concentrations in the atmosphere. The Kyoto Protocol, adopted in 1997, refined the convention. It obligates industrialized countries to attain legally binding GHG emission targets during the period 2008–2012, which are on average 5 per cent below 1990 GHG emission levels. The protocol is expected to enter into force in 2003 following ratification by the requisite number of parties.

The Kyoto Protocol allows developed countries to meet part of their emission reduction obligations abroad, based on the principle of achieving GHG emission reductions where costs are lowest. The protocol provides for market-based mechanisms that could potentially fund emission reduction measures, as covered by Article 4.2 of the UNFCCC. One, the Clean Development Mechanism (CDM), allows developed countries to finance GHG reduction projects in developing countries and provides for generation and transfer of 'certified emission reductions' (CER).

Developing countries like Afghanistan are presently under no obligation to constrain their GHG emissions, but may, on a voluntary basis, contribute to global emission reductions by hosting projects under the CDM. The principal goals of the CDM are to assist host developing countries in achieving sustainable development with respect to GHG emissions, at the same time enabling them to benefit from abatement projects, and to help industrialized countries in achieving their emission reduction targets.

CER will be issued corresponding to the emission reductions achieved. Industrialized countries may use CER accruing from CDM projects as contributions towards compliance with part of their emission reduction commitments under the protocol. It is anticipated that CER will be bought and sold in a new environmental market established under the Kyoto Protocol.

Afghanistan has the chance to benefit from the CDM by:

- attracting additional capital for projects that contribute to a more prosperous but less carbon-intensive economy;

- encouraging and permitting active participation by both the private and public sectors;

- obtaining technology transfer; and

- defining investment priorities that meet sustainable development goals.

In order to participate in the CDM, there are certain eligibility criteria that countries must meet. These include ratification of the Kyoto Protocol and the establishment of a national CDM focal point. The host country government has a central role to play in deciding on the nature and scope of CDM-projects and on the allocation of the property rights over GHG emission reductions. Elements for a successful CDM programme include policy and regulation, capacity building activities, and appropriate institutions.

The following rules and conditions must be fulfilled by CDM-projects:

- The project shall lead to real, measurable and long-term emission reductions, certified by a third-party agency;

- The emission reductions achieved must be additional to any emission reductions that would have occurred without the project;

- With respect to forests, only afforestation and reforestation activities are attributable under CDM, but not forest management and conservation;

- The project must be in line with sustainable development objectives defined by the host government;

- Projects starting from 2000 onwards are eligible for generating CERs;

- Baseline validation and registration, emission reduction monitoring and reporting, and verification and certification of CER are obligatory;

- CDM projects shall not be funded from a diversion of Official Development Assistance (but ODA funds may be used for capacity building);

- Projects must be approved by the CDM Executive Board of the Parties of the UNFCCC.

The unilateral CDM approach may represent the most realistic way for Afghanistan to benefit from its GHG reduction potential. Once the first CDM projects have been registered and the first CER generated, it will be comparatively easy for the Afghan government to find international buyers willing to pay for immediate delivery of CERs.

Part of the costs involved in approving and implementing CDM projects are independent of project size and reduce the perceived CER value of smaller CDM projects. The Marrakesh Accords recognized this problem and proposed the development of simplified procedures for small-scale CDM projects that can offer CERs at competitive prices.

Several countries have recently engaged in CDM-type emission reduction projects that are likely to generate CERs. One pioneer is the Prototype Carbon Fund, a US$180 million facility established by the World Bank. Typical prices for carbon credits range from US$3 to US$5 per ton of CO_2 equivalent. Another market pioneer is the Dutch government which is paying similar prices for CERs. In addition, several commercial funds have announced their intention to generate CERs.

CO_2 emissions in Afghanistan – energy, fuel and forestry sectors

Based on information collected in Afghanistan, UNEP was able to estimate CO_2 emissions, in terms of tons per year per person, as 0.01 from electricity production, 0.1 from fuel consumption and 1 from unsustainable fuelwood consumption. It is thus evident that the future mitigation potential in Afghanistan lies not in the reduction of actual emissions from electricity production and transportation but in two directions:

- the replacement of fuelwood, in part, with renewable energy alternatives such as solar, hydro and wind power;

- the replacement of future electricity, industry and transportation development concepts with GHG friendly technologies under the CDM.

To demonstrate the benefits of the CDM as a means for project financing, a number of possibilities are given in the table below. The projects are either based on priorities in the Afghan National Development Framework or on concepts by UNEP.

Table 1. CDM opportunities for Afghanistan

Afforestation Program	
Short description	Afforestation of 10 000 ha of degraded semi-arid soils. Annual plantings of about 1 200 ha between 2005 and 2012, with about 500-1 000 plants per hectare.
Baseline assumption	Baseline stock is defined as the carbon stock generated on the land either naturally or artificially in the absence of the project activity. Estimated CO2 equestration during the first commitment period with a mean area afforested of 8 000 ha.
ESTIMATED GREENHOUSE GAS BENEFIT:	**72,000 t CO_2 / year**

Large hydro power plants > 15 MW (Example Koner River plant, 1 GW)	
Short description	Installation or rehabilitation of hydro power plants (> 15MW), partly in combination with irrigation systems for the electrification of Afghanistan. Example: serves the Koner River plant with the annual electricity production capacity of 6330 GWh.
Baseline assumption	Assumptions: 33% of power will be generated by gas, 33% by diesel and crude oil and 33% by coal: 600 t CO_2 / GWh
ESTIMATED GREENHOUSE GAS BENEFIT:	**3.8 Mio t CO_2 / year**

Small Scale Hydro Power < 15 MW	
Short description	New installation or rehabilitation of small hydropower plants, partly in combination with irrigation systems, bundled for CDM purposes to a 15 MW package with 6 330 hours annual operation.
Baseline assumption	0.8 kg CO_2 equ /kWh (see table B-4, Load factor 25%, Annex B, Attachment 3 Marrakesh Accords)
ESTIMATED GREENHOUSE GAS BENEFIT:	**76,000 t CO_2 / year**

Wind Power	
Short description	Power production with wind power turbines in a 15 MW wind park (Small Scale CDM) with 3750 hours of annual operation.
Baseline assumption	0.8 kg CO_2 equ /kWh (see table B-4,Load factor 25%,Annex B,Attachment 3 Marrakesh Accords)
ESTIMATED GREENHOUSE GAS BENEFIT:	**45,000 t CO_2 / year**

Light Bulb Program for 100'000 Families	
Short description	Energy saving light bulbs do need less electricity (minus 80%). The 100'000 family program shall supply 4 lamps with 8 W per family intstead of 4 times 40 W, the total amount of supplied energy saving light bulbs will be 400'000.
Baseline assumption	Assumptions: 33% of electric power will be generated by gas, 33% by diesel and crude oil and 33% by coal: 600 t CO_2 / GWh
ESTIMATED GREENHOUSE GAS BENEFIT:	**8,400 t CO_2/ year**

Solar Cooking Program for 10'000 Families	
Short description	Parabolic concentrators produce hot steam or hot water by using solar power. Today cooking uses gas (from Uzbekistan), diesel burners and wood. The 10'000 family program will support 1 cooker per family, which leads to 10'000 cooking units in total.
Baseline assumption	An average family uses 4 t of firewood per year. Solar cookers cannot operate all year round, therefore it is assumed that half of the energy, respectively 2 t/yr, will still come from firewood. The emissions of 2 t unsustainable burned wood are 3.6 t CO_2/yr.
ESTIMATED GREENHOUSE GAS BENEFIT:	**36,000 t CO_2/ year**

Wind Water Pumping	
Short description	Wind turbines with a total capacity of 15MW are connected to pumping units for irrigation or drinking water.
Baseline assumption	The renewable generating unit may be new or replace an existing fossil fuel fired source of mechanical power with 0.8 kg CO_2equ /kWh (see table B-2 and B-4, Load factor 50%, Annex B, Attachment 3 Marrakesh Accords)
ESTIMATED GREENHOUSE GAS BENEFIT:	**45,000 t CO_2/ year**

Solar Hot Water Program for 10'000 Families	
Short description	Provision of solar hot water and heating facilities for 10'000 families. Water flows through pipes on the roof and are heated by the sun, instead of hot water produced with wood, gas or diesel burners. The 10'000 family program will supply 2000 litres of hot water per family per year, which leads to 20 Mio. litres hot water.
Baseline assumption	1.5 t CO_2 per 100 litres of hot water lead to 30 t CO_2 per family and year.
ESTIMATED GREENHOUSE GAS BENEFIT: 300,000 t CO_2 / YEAR	**300,000 t CO_2/ year**

Post-Conflict Environmental Assessment

Annex B

Laboratory analyses and sample results

AFGHANISTAN

Table 1. Water quality samples, urban environments

Sample no.	Sampling Site	E. Coli 100 ml	Total Coliform 100 ml	Nitrate mg/l	Chloride mg/l	Ammonium mg/l	pH	Conductivity µS/cm
Herat 3	Drinking water, deep well at hospital	5/100	0/100	25	na	na	7.5	950
Herat 4	Tap water, Hospital operation room	1/100	0/100	50	75	na	8.0	1040
Herat 5	Drinking water, hospital shallow well	9/100	13/100	50	75	na	8.0	1320
Herat 9	Drinking water, shallow well near oil storage	> d.l.	> d.l.	10	40	na	6.5	640
Herat 13	Sewer water at outfall	na	na	0	na	> 0.8	7.5	na
Kab 3a	Kabul river, surface water	> d.l.	> d.l.	0	na	> 0.8	8.0	na
Kab 3b	Effluent from WWTP	> d.l.	> d.l.	0	na	> 0.8	8.0	na
Kab 5	Drinking water, shallow well (25 m) in District 6	23/100	> d.l.	0	na	na	7.0	na
Kab 6	Drinking water, shallow well (13-14 m) in District 6	18/100	> d.l.	0	na	na	7.0	na
Kab 8	Drinking water, shallow well near oil storage	> d.l.	> d.l.	na	na	na	na	na
Kab 10	UNICA guest house, kitchen	2/100	> d.l.	25	150	na	7.5	1000
Kab 11	UNICA guest house, water filter container	0/100	> d.l.	25	150	na	7.0	800
Kab 12	UNICA guest house, bottled water	0/100	10/100	25	150	na	7.0	810
Kand 1	Tap water, Hospital Laboratory	0/100	0/100	na	na	na	na	na
Kand 2	Tap water, Hospital Kitchen	0/100	0/100	50	na	na	na	na
Kand 3	Drinking water, shallow well	0/100	0/100	25	na	na	6.5	1070
Kand 4	Irrigation water, shallow well near oil storage	0/100	4/100	0	na	na	7.0	730
Mazar 1	Shallow drinking water well, mosque	9/100	0/100	50	40	na	7.0	na
Mazar 2	River water, down stream from fertilizer	na	na	0	na	0.2	na	na
Mazar 3	Drinking water from public tap	38/100	28/100	250	150	na	7.0	1800
Mazar 4	River water, down stream from crude oil terminal	> d.l.	> d.l.	0	na	na	7.0	na
Mazar 5	Shallow water well, Shiburghan	8/100	> d.l.	10	na	na	7.5	1620
Mazar 8	Shallow drinking water well, along river	1/100	> d.l.	0	40	na	7.0	1360
Mazar 9	Drinking water, water treatment plant	1/100	0/100	25	na	na	7.5	450
Mazar 10	Wastewater from textile factory	na	na	0	na	na	8.0	2300
Mazar 11	Shallow drinking water well, hospital	1/100	30/100	50	75	na	7.0	1540
Mazar 12	Tap water, hospital operation room	2/100	50/100	50	75	na	7.0	1150

na = not analysed; > d.l. = Above detection limit (>100 counts of bacteria in 100 ml of water)

Post-Conflict Environmental Assessment

Table 2. Water quality samples, Helmand and Amu Darya basins

Sample No.	Sampling Site	GPS Easting	GPS Northing	Chloride mg/l	pH	Conductivity (20 C) S/cm
K1	Lalalan village, between Kabul and Qalat. Exit from karez into pool for irrigation.	67.88120°	32.01880°	8.3	8.00	333
K2	Helmand, Kajaki dam outlet being released for irrigation.	65.11610°	32.32350°	7.6	7.91	343
K3	Gershk, Boghra Canal from Helmand River	64.56030°	31.81050°	11	8.18	388
K4	Village of Khash Rud on Delaram to Gor Gorrie track. Water from well, water table at depth 7m.	62.88440°	31.66010°	115	7.69	1,070
K5	Zaranj. Well sample at 3m from MDM compound. Brackish, muddy supply no longer in use.	61° 51' 50"	30° 57' 40"	5,320	7.18	23,400
K6	N. of Zaranj. Kang area. Local govt. centre. Interviews with officials. Well, saline not used for DWS, w/t at 1. 5m.	61.82010°	31.16920°	16,000	7.57	50,500
K7	N. of Zaranj. Kang area. Village of Irrigation Dept, official. Large hand dug sump well 7 m deep. Used for irrigation of garden.	61.83800°	31.19200°	85	7.98	1,370
K8	Bed of Helmand River. Wind blown sands, eroded recent river alluvium - silts, sand & gravel. Water sample from well, w/t 2m depth. Location at start of Lashkari Canal, south of Zaranj.	61.81500°	30.61920°	482	7.96	2,880
K9	Left bank of Helmand River at Nazir, 12km west of Char Burjak. Village on +5m terrace adjacent to cliffs of ancient silts with gravel cap. Water from well, w/t at 5.5m, rises in spring.	62.01070°	30.26250°	297	7.60	2,150
K10	Zaranj. UNHCR Field Centre. Water sample taken from tap.	61° 51' 55"	30° 57' 44"	93	8.17	968
K11	Kota Lak. Water sample from watercourse I km SW from off-take on Khash Rud base flow.	63° 05' 20"	31° 53' 30"	66	8.10	742
K12	Delaram and Khash Rud. Water sample from floor of the Khash Rud base flow.	63.42750°	32.16500°	12	8.05	370
K13	Gor Gorrie. Center of town. Water sample from well at 13m depth	62.63060°	31.44730°	172	7.79	1,230
M1	Well, on desert plain, road to Peace Bridge. Recently dug well where farmer hopes irrigation. W/t at 12m	67° 18' 30"	37° 01' 30"	647	7.72	3,100
M2	Amu Darya River. Site on bank with Tamarix and irrigated fields. Some stream bank erosion. River 1.5 below bank.	67° 13' 30"	37° 12' 00"	54	7.13	587
M3	Saline have been borrow-pits for bricks. Saline vegetation and salt crusts pools on edge of alluvium up to dunes, and origin may. Water table at 1m.	67° 15' 00"	37° 09' 00"	19,900	9.06	65,900
M4	Brick kiln at largely ruined settlement 4 km north of Aqcha town. Silty soils here have long been used for bricks. W/t at 13m.	66° 10' 30"	36° 56' 00"	186	7.56	3,280
M5	Well Mengel Zek, N of Aqchah. w/t at 10m, was at 8m four years ago. Also fluctuates during year by ± 1m; locals said it is slightly salty.	66° 08' 00"	37° 01' 10"	373	7.55	4,070
M6	Public hand pump, Aqchah. Part of town supply. Depth w/t approx. 25m.	66° 11' 00"	36° 54' 00'	331	7.45	4,010
M7	Aqchah irrigation canal. 7 km south of town centre. Low flow about 30 l/s.	66° 12' 40"	36° 51' 10"	108	8.33	1,030
M8	Hot spring, NE of Mazar-e-Sharif. Approx. 30 l/ sec. artesian flow from tubewell. Hot water > 50° C, with deposition of sulphur & calcium carbonate. Former health spa and sanatorium.	67° 20' 40"	36° 54' 10"	1,260	7.89	6,370
M9	Well, UNAMA, Mazar-e-Sharif, typical of town supply. Depth to w/t said to be 19m.	67° 06' 50"	36° 41' 50"	98	7.75	1,360

GPS = Global Positioning System; w/t = Water table; Salinity Classes (FAO Guidelines for water quality for irrigation): EC <750mS/cm = No problem; EC 750-3 000mS/cm = Increasing problem; EC >3 000mS/cm = Severe Problem

Table 3. Water samples for hydrocarbon contaminants

Sample no	Sampling Site	Total Hydrocarbons mg/l	Alphatic Hydrocarbons (Sum C5-C10) µg/l	Methylen Chloride µg/l	Toluene µg/l	Alkane (Sum C5-C10) µg/l
Herat 3	Drinking water, deep well at hospital	< 0.02				
Herat 9	Drinking water, shallow well near oil storage	0.05				
Kab 2	Oil-Reloading	< 0.02				
Kab 8	Drinking water, shallow well near oil storage	< 0.02				
Kand 4	Irrigation water, shallow well near oil storage	< 0.02	< 10	0.08	32	< 10
Mazar 4	River water, down stream from crude oil terminal	< 0.02				
Mazar 9	Drinking water, water treatment plant	< 0.02				

Table 4. Soil samples for hydrocarbon contaminants

Sample no.	Sampling Site	Total hydrocarbons mg/kg TS	Poly-aromatic Hydrocarbons (PAHs)
Herat 6	Underground oil storage at the Hospital	135,000	
Herat 7	Oil storage at the Hospital	826,000	
Herat 8	Oil storage in Mawlawy	46,000	
Kab 1	Oil-Reloading	123,000	
Kand 5	Soil under transformer station	60,000	
Mazar 6	Private oil refinery	83,000	Indications

Post-Conflict Environmental Assessment

Table 5. Identification of chemical components

Sample no. Sample description		Herat 12 Dust from the battery recycling room at Zuri Battery factory	Kab 4 Salt used in shoe production	Kab 9 Powder used for food dying	Mazar 7 Oil sludge from private oil refinery	Mazar 13 Plastic granulate from plastic recycling
Lead	g/kg	300 - 400				
Antimony	g/kg	10				
Arsenic	g/kg	0.6				
Copper	g/kg	0.2				11
Zinc	g/kg	0.4	0.020			28
Chromium (Cr6+)	g/kg		< 0.005			
Iron	g/kg		1.2	0.280		0.090
Lithium	g/kg		0.060			
Titanium	g/kg		0.030			
Barium	g/kg		0.030			20
Bromide	g/kg			0.030		
Strontium	g/kg			0.320		0.300
Sulphur	g/kg				99 ±3	

Table 6. Composition of different oil products

Sample no. Sampling site:	Herat 10 Tar factory	Herat 11 Tar factory	Kab 7 Transformer oil at Power station	Kand 5 Transformer station at Vielko Dam
Organic parameters: Sum PAH	487 mg/kg	2 6 mg/kg		
Benzo(a)pyren	<5 mg/kg	<5 mg/kg		
Naphthalin	383 mg/kg	8.6 mg/kg		
Acenaphthylen	<0.05 mg/kg	<0.05 mg/kg		
Acenaphthen	92 mg/kg	5.8 mg/kg		
Fluoren	12 mg/kg	<0.05 mg/kg		
Phenanthren	<0.05 mg/kg	5.7 mg/kg		
Anthracen	<0.05 mg/kg	<0.05 mg/kg		
Fluoranthen	<0.05 mg/kg	<0.05 mg/kg		
Pyren	<0.05 mg/kg	5.83 mg/kg		
Chrysen	<0.05 mg/kg	<0.05 mg/kg		
Benzo(a)anthracen	<0.05 mg/kg	<0.05 mg/kg		
Benzo(b)fluoranthen	<0.05 mg/kg	<0.05 mg/kg		
Benzo(k)fluoranthen	<0.05 mg/kg	<0.05 mg/kg		
Benzo(a)pyren	<0.05 mg/kg	<0.05 mg/kg		
Indeno(1,2,3-cd)pyren	<0.05 mg/kg	<0.05 mg/kg		
Dibenzo(a,h)anthracen	<0.05 mg/kg	<0.05 mg/kg		
Benzo(g,h,i)perylen	<0.05 mg/kg	<0.05 mg/kg		
PCB 28			—	0.002 mg/kg
PCB 52			—	0.005mg/kg
PCB 101			—	0.005 mg/kg
PCB 118			—	0.010mg/kg
PCB 138			—	<0.002 mg/kg
PCB 153			—	<0.002 mg/kg
PCB 180			—	<0.002 mg/kg
PCB Sum n.AHR; AltIV			< 25 mg/kg	0.05 mg/kg

AFGHANISTAN

Table 7. Air samples

Sample no. Sampling site: Sampling time (h): Sampling volume (m³):	006 Herat Hospital 8.3 187	003 Kabul MoPH 6.5 146	004 Kabul UNICA 0.4 9	001 Kandahar Hospital 0.7 16	002 Kandahar ICRC 0.4 9	005 Mazar Municip. 6.3 142	007 Mazar Centre 0.5 11
Naphtalene	< 0.01	0.02	0.02	< 0.01	0.03	0.02	< 0.01
Acenaphthylene	< 0.01	< 0.01	< 0.01	< 0.01	< 0.01	< 0.01	< 0.01
Acenaphthene	< 0.01	0.04	0.02	0.03	0.04	< 0.01	< 0.01
Fluorene	< 0.01	< 0.01	< 0.01	< 0.01	0.04	< 0.01	< 0.01
Phenanthrene	0.07	0.15	0.16	0.12	0.26	0.11	0.09
Anthracene	< 0.01	< 0.01	< 0.01	< 0.01	< 0.01	0.12	< 0.01
Fluoranthene	0.05	0.17	0.12	0.07	0.10	< 0.01	0.09
Pyrene	0.03	0.07	0.04	0.02	0.02	0.05	0.06
Chrysene	0.08	0.04	0.01	< 0.01	< 0.01	< 0.01	0.32
Benzo(a)anthracene	0.01	0.04	0.01	0.01	< 0.01	0.01	0.06
Benzo(b)fluoranthene	0.12	0.22	0.09	0.06	0.04	0.30	0.29
Benzo(k)fluoranthene	0.09	0.17	0.08	0.04	0.04	0.13	0.23
Benzo(a)pyrene	0.05	0.13	0.05	0.04	0.03	0.26	0.15
Indeno(1,2,3-cd)pyrene	0.12	0.19	0.09	0.04	0.04	0.23	0.15
Dibenzo(a,h)anthracene	0.03	0.07	0.01	< 0.01	< 0.01	< 0.01	0.09
Benzo(g,h,i)perylene	0.14	0.21	0.09	0.04	0.04	< 0.01	0.20
Sum of PAH	0.79	1.5	0.8	0.47	0.67	1.2	1.7
PAH-rounded value (ng/m³)	5	10	90	30	70	10	150

Post-Conflict Environmental Assessment

Table 8. Soil samples for pesticide contamination

Parameters (mg/kg)	Silt sample Zaranj	Reed beds Zaranj	Dust Zaranj
alpha-HCH	<0.01	<0.01	<0.01
beta-HCH	<0.01	<0.01	<0.01
gamma-HCH	<0.01	<0.01	<0.01
delta-HCH	<0.01	<0.01	<0.01
epsilon-HCH	<0.01	<0.01	<0.01
Hexachlorbenzol	<0.01	<0.01	<0.01
Heptachlor	<0.01	<0.01	<0.01
cis-Heptachlorapoxide	<0.01	<0.01	<0.01
trans-Heptachlorepoxide	<0.01	<0.01	<0.01
methoxychlor	<0.01	<0.01	<0.01
Mirex	<0.01	<0.01	<0.01
Aldrin	<0.01	<0.01	<0.01
Dieldrin	<0.01	0.02	0.02
Endrin	<0.01	<0.01	<0.01
Isodrin	<0.01	<0.01	<0.01
oxy-Chlordane	<0.01	<0.01	<0.01
cis-Chlordane	<0.01	<0.01	<0.01
trans-Chlordane	<0.01	<0.01	<0.01
alpha-Endosulfan	<0.01	<0.01	<0.01
beta-Endosulfan	<0.01	<0.01	<0.01
o,p'-DDE	<0.01	<0.01	<0.01
p,p'-DDE	<0.01	<0.01	<0.01
o,p'-DDD	<0.01	<0.01	<0.01
o,p'-DDD	<0.01	<0.01	<0.01
o,p'-DDT	<0.01	<0.01	<0.01
o,p'-DDT	<0.01	<0.01	<0.01
Sum of organochloropesticides	<0.01	<0.03	<0.03

Annex C

Additional field mission photos

Forest assessment team

UNEP, 2002

Protected areas
assessment team

UNEP, 2002

Urban assessment team

UNEP, 2002

Wakhan Corridor
assessment team

Water basins
assessment team

Kabul office staff

AFGHANISTAN

C Urban

DENNIS BRUHN/UNEP.2002

Women washing clothes in the Kabul River

DENNIS BRUHN/UNEP.2002

Vegetable stand above open sewer

DENNIS BRUHN/UNEP.2002

View of Kabul

Post-Conflict Environmental Assessment

DENNIS BRUHN/UNEP.2002

Local waterway in
Kandahar

SANDRA PANIGA/UNEP.2002

Kandahar hospital

SØREN HVILSHØJ/UNEP.2002

UNEP water
samples taken
from well in
Kandahar

AFGHANISTAN

C Forests

Limited evidence of natural regeneration near Narop

MARTYN MURRAY/UNEP, 2002

Distant mountains contain the pistachio forests of Farkhar village

DAVID JENSEN/UNEP, 2002

Extensive grazing tracks in pistachio woodland near Farkhar village

MARTYN MURRAY/UNEP, 2002

Post-Conflict Environmental Assessment

DAVID JENSEN/UNEP, 2002

Evidence of porcupine damage on pistachio tree

MARTYN MURRAY/UNEP, 2002

Cedar beam in Jalalabad timber market

AFGHANISTAN

Water basins

Registan desert encroaching on farmland

RENE NIJENHUIS/UNEP, 2002

Well dug for irrigation in Sistan wetlands

RENE NIJENHUIS/UNEP, 2002

Former wetland area in Sistan basin

RENE NIJENHUIS/UNEP, 2002

Post-Conflict Environmental Assessment

RENE NIJENHUIS/UNEP, 2002

Karez system near Ghanzi

RENE NIJENHUIS/UNEP, 2002

Water pump in empty canal in Sistan wetlands

AFGHANISTAN

161

Protected areas

KOEN TOONEN/UNEP, 2002

View of the
Bamiyan valley

CHRIS SHANK/UNEP, 2002

Severe erosion
west of Bamiyan
town

CHRIS SHANK/UNEP, 2002

Travertine dam
between Bande
Panir and Bande
Haibat,
Band-e-Amir

CHRIS SHANK/UNEP, 2002

Flour mills at base of Bande Haibat dam

CHRIS SHANK/UNEP, 2002

Typical house enclosure at Band-e-Amir

CHRIS SHANK/UNEP, 2002

Spring-fed ponds at Dasht-e-Nawar

C

Wakhan Corridor

ANTHONY FITZHERBERT/UNEP, 2002

Traditional yurt, Ishtemich valley

ANTHONY FITZHERBERT/UNEP, 2002

Afghan guide displaying Marco Polo sheep skull, Ishtemich valley

ANTHONY FITZHERBERT/UNEP, 2002

Herders, Ishtemich valley

Post-Conflict Environmental Assessment

CHARUDUTT MISHRA/UNEP, 2002

Camel, Sarhad-e-Broghil area

CHARUDUTT MISHRA/UNEP, 2002

Looking across Pamir River to Tajikistan, Porsan valley

ANTHONY FITZHERBERT/UNEP, 2002

UNEP mission on horseback, Chap Kol lake

AFGHANISTAN

C

Legacy of war

PETER ZAHLER/UNEP, 2002

Destroyed tank near Bamiyan

UNEP, 2002

Outpost in Kunar

Unexploded ordinance in Bamiyan province (left) and Farkhar (right)

PETER ZAHLER/UNEP, 2002

MARTYN MURRAY/UNEP, 2002

PETER ZAHLER/UNEP, 2002

Land mine poster, Band-e-Amir

RENE NIJENHUIS/UNEP, 2002

Bombed truck en route to Qalat

LUKE POWELL, 2002

Partially uncovered landmine near Kabul

AFGHANISTAN

Aerial views of the Hindu Kush

UNEP, 2002

UNEP, 2002

UNEP, 2002

Post-Conflict Environmental Assessment

Annex D
Literature cited

1. Future Harvest Consortium to Rebuild Agriculture in Afghanistan (Future Harvest). 2002a. *Needs assessment on feeds, livestock and rangelands in Afghanistan*. Draft. Coordinated by the International Centre for Agricultural Research in the Dry Areas (ICARDA). Cornwall. Available (November 2002) at http://www.icarda.org/ Afghanistan/Live_NA-Chapter_1-7.pdf

2. United Nations Office on Drugs and Crime (UNODC). 2000. *United Nations Drug Control Programme (UNDCP) opium poppy survey in Afghanistan*. Newsletter Issue November 1, 2002. Vienna. Available (December 2002) at http://www.undcp.org/ odccp/newsletter_2000-11-01_1_page006.html

3. *Ibid.*

4. United Nations Drug Control Programme (UNDCP). 2001. *Annual opium poppy survey 2001*. Vienna. Available (November 2002) at http://www.undcp.org/pdf/afg/ report_2001-10-16_1.pdf

5. United Nations Drug Control Programme (UNDCP). 2002. *Annual opium poppy survey 2002*. Vienna.

6. Future Harvest. 2002a.

7. World Bank. 1999. *Role and Size of Livestock Sector in Afghanistan*. Washington. Available (December 2002) at http://lnweb18.worldbank.org/SAR/sa.nsf/ Attachments/95/$File/afLvstk.pdf

8. *Ibid.*

9. *Ibid.*

10. *Ibid.*

11. United Nations Secretariat, Department of Economic and Social affairs, Population Division. 2001a. *World Population Prospects: The 2000 Revision and World Urbanization Prospects: The 2001 Revision*. New York

12. United Nations High Commissioner for Refugees (UNHCR). 2002. *Assisted Voluntary Repatriation Summary Report – October 31st 2002*. Geneva. Available (December 2002) at http://www.hic.org.pk/assistance_sectors/refugee/ assisted_voluntary_repatriation_summary_report_october_2002.pdf

13. *Ibid.*

14. United Nations Secretariat, Department of Economic and Social affairs, Population Division. 2000. *Afghanistan*. New York.

15. United Nations Children's Fund (UNICEF). 2002. *Maternal Mortality in Afghanistan: Magnitude, Causes, Risk Factors and Preventability*. New York. Available (December 2002) at http://www.unicef.org/media/publications/ maternalmortalityafghanistan.doc

16. United Nations Children's Fund (UNICEF). 2001. *State of the World's Children 2001*. New York. Available (December 2002) at http://www.unicef.org/sowc01/pdf/fullsowc.pdf

17. Future Harvest. 2002a.

18. Asian Development Bank (ADB). 2002. *Afghanistan: Initial Country Strategy and Program 2002-2004*. Manila. Available (November 2002) at http://www.adb.org/Documents/CSPs/AFG/2002/csp0100.asp

19. Kapos, V., J. Rhind, M. Edwards, M.F. Price and C. Ravilious. 2000. Developing a map of the world's mountain forests In M.F. Price and N. Butt (eds.) *Forests in sustainable mountain development: A state-of-knowledge report for 2000*. CAB International, Wallingford.

20. Food and Agricultural Organization (FAO). 1981. *National Parks and Wildlife Management, Afghanistan. A contribution to a conservation strategy*. Based on the work of J.A. Sayer and A.P.M. van der Zon. Vol. 1, text. FO:DP/AFG/78/007. Rome.

21. World Conservation Union (IUCN). 2002. *IUCN Red list of Threatened Species*. IUCN Species Survival Commission. Gland. Available (December 2002) at http://www.redlist.org/

22. BirdLife International. 2000. World Bird Database. *Record for Siberian Crane*. Cambridge. Available (December 2002) at http://www.birdlife.net/species/species_search.cfm

23. Convention on Migratory Species (CMS). 2002. *Conservation Plan for the Central Population of Siberian Cranes*. Bonn. Available (December 2002) at http://www.savingcranes.org/SCFC/gefmaps/ConsPlan%20_CP_website.doc

24. United Nations Office for the Coordination of Humanitarian Affairs (UNOCHA). 2002a. *Afghanistan: More than two million return home this year*. Geneva. Available (December 2002) at http://www.reliefweb.int/w/rwb.nsf/VOCHARUAllLatestEmergencyReports/C34F620D04CB927185256CA000598280?OpenDocument

25. UNHCR. 2002.

26. FAO. 1981.

27. Food and Agricultural Organization (FAO). 1977a. *A strategy for the establishment and development of Band-e-Amir National Park*. Prepared by C. Shank and J. Larsson. FO:/DP/AFG/74/016 Field Document 8. Rome.

28. Food and Agricultural Organization (FAO). 1978a. *A preliminary study of Lake Hashmat Khan with recommendations for management*. Prepared by A. Rahim and J.Y. Larson. FO:DP/AFG/74/016. 17 pp. Field Document No. 10. Rome.

29. Food and Agricultural Organization (FAO). 1977b. *Management plan for Ab-i-Estada and Dashte Nawar Flamingo and Waterfowl Sanctuaries*. Prepared by C. Shank and W. F. Rodenburg. FO:DP/AFG/74/016 Field Document. Rome.

30. Food and Agricultural Organization (FAO). 1977c. *A Preliminary Management Plan for the Ajar Valley Wildlife Reserve*. Prepared by C. Shank, R.G. Petocz, and K. Habibi. FO: DP/AFG/74/016 Field Document. Rome.

31. Food and Agricultural Organization (FAO). 1978b. *Report on the Afghan Pamir*. Prepared by R. Petocz, K. Habibi, A. Jamil and A. Wassey. FAO:DP/AFG/74/016/ Field Document No. 6. Rome.

32. Food and Agricultural Organization (FAO). 1977d. *The trade in wild animal furs in Afghanistan*. Prepared by W.F. Rodenburg. FO:DP/AFG/74/016 Field Document. Rome.

33. Food and Agricultural Organization (FAO). 1977e. *Ecological reconnaissance of western Nuristan for management*. Prepared by R. G. Petocz and J.Y. Larsson. FO:DP/AFG/ 74/016 Field Document. Rome.

34. Food and Agricultural Organization (FAO). 1977f. *The mammals of Afghanistan and their distribution*. Prepared by H. Habibi. FAO:DP/AFG/74/016 Field Document. Rome.

35. Save the Environment Afghanistan (SEA). 2000. *The Status of the Environment in Afghanistan*. Prepared by A.N. Ahmadi, A.W. Modaqiq, A. Khairzad, A.G. Ghoryani, and G.M. Malikyar. Kabul.

36. Saba, D. 2001. Afghanistan: Environmental degradation in a fragile ecological setting. *International Journal of Sustainable Development and World Ecology*. Volume 8: 279-289.

37. FAO. 1977a.

38. FAO. 1978a.

39. Food and Agricultural Organization (FAO). 1997. *AQUASTAT Afghanistan Country Profile*. Rome. Available (November 2002) at Http://www.fao.org/waicent/faoinfo/ agricult/agl/aglw/aquastat/countries/afghanistan/index.stm

40. Future Harvest Consortium to Rebuild Agriculture in Afghanistan (Future Harvest). 2002b. *Seed and crop improvement situation assessment, April-May 2002*. Coordinated by the International Centre for Agricultural Research in the Dry Areas (ICARDA). Cornwall. Available (December 2002) at http://www.icarda.org/Afghanistan/NA/ fsummary.htm

41. Partow, H. 2003. Sistan Oasis Parched by Drought. In *Atlas of Global Change*. United Nations Environment Programme. Oxford University Press (in preparation), Oxford.

42. Tate, G.P. 1909. *The frontiers of Baluchistan. Travels on the borders of Persia and Afghanistan*. Witherby & Co., London. Reprinted 1976 by East and West Publishing Company, Lahore.

43. Convention on Wetlands of International Importance especially as Waterfowl Habitat (Ramsar). 2002. *Ramsar List of Wetlands of International Importance*. Gland.

44. FAO. 1981.

45. Partow. 2003.

46. *Ibid*.

47. Christensen, P. 1998. Middle Eastern irrigation: legacies and lessons. *Yale Forestry & Environmental Science Bulletin* 103: 15-30. Available (November 2002) at http:// www.yale.edu/environment/publications/bulletin/103pdfs/103christensen.pdf

48. United Nations. 2001a. *United Nations Inter-agency Assessment Report on the Extreme Drought in the Islamic Republic of Iran*. Tehran, Islamic Republic of Iran, July 2001.

49. *Ibid*.

50. Partow. 2003.

51. *Ibid*.

52. Aitchison, J.E.T. 1888. Botany of the Afghan Delimitation Commission. *Trans. Linn. Soc.* Series 2, Botany. Vol III, London.

53. United Nations. 2001a.

54. Global Resource Information Database (GRID). 2001. *Amu Darya*. http://www.grida.no/enrin/htmls/uzbek/env2001/content/soe/english/amudar.htm

55. United Nations Economic Commission for Europe. 2000. Management of selected problems in the Aral and Caspian Sea regions in *Environmental Performance Reviews – Kazakhstan*. Geneva.

56. Future Harvest Consortium to Rebuild Agriculture in Afghanistan (Future Harvest). 2002c. *Draft Needs Assessment on Soil and Water in Afghanistan*. Coordinated by the International Center for Agricultural Research in the Dry Areas (ICARDA). Cornwall. 2002. Available (December 2002) at http://www.icarda.org/Afghanistan/NA/NA_SoilWater.pdf

57. Integrated Regional Information Network (IRIN). 2001. *Focus on locust infestation in Northern Afghanistan*. 28 June 2001. Available (December 2002) at http://www.irinnews.org/report.asp?ReportID=8909&SelectRegion=Central_Asia

58. Food and Agricultural Organization (FAO). 2002. Afghanistan: *Locust control campaign successfully concluded*. 1 August 2002. Rome. Available (December 2002) at http://www.fao.org/english/newsroom/news/2002/7880-en.html

59. World Conservation Union (IUCN). 1991. *Opportunities for Improved Environmental Management in Afghanistan*. By N. MacPherson and B.K. Fernando. Gland.

60. United Nations Office for the Coordination of Humanitarian Affairs (UNOCHA). 2002b. Transitional Assistance Programme for Afghanistan January 2003 to March 2004. Geneva. Available (December 2002) at http://www.reliefweb.int/appeals/2003/files/tapa03.pdf

61. Vinogradov, S. and V.P.E. Langford. 2001. *Managing transboundary water resources in the Aral Sea Basin: in search of a solution*. International Journal of Global Environmental Issues, Vol. 1, Nos. 3/4, 2001. Available (December 2002) at http://www.internationalwaterlaw.org/Bibliography/IJGEI/07ijgenvl2001v1n34vinogradov.pdf

62. World Commission on Dams. 2000. *Development and dams – a new framework for decision-making. The report of the World Commission on Dams*. Earthscan Publications Limited, London.

63. FAO. 1981.

64. *Ibid*.

Post-Conflict Environmental Assessment

65. Food and Agricultural Organization (FAO). 1993. *Land Cover Map of the Islamic State of Afghanistan*. 1:250,000 scale. Rome.

66. FAO. 1981.

67. FAO. 1977a.

68. *Ibid.*

69. FAO. 1978a.

70. *Ibid.*

71. FAO. 1977b.

72. *Ibid.*

73. *Ibid..*

74. *Ibid.*

75. *Ibid.*

76. Khan, A. 2002. *Impact of exotic technology on Physical Environment and Cultural Practices in Ab-i-Estada*. (Unpublished). Submitted to Geography Department, University of Wisconsin, USA.

77. Sauey, R. 1985. *The Range, status, and winter ecology of the Siberian Crane (Grus leucogeranus)*. Ph. D. diss. Cornell University, Ithaca, New York.

78. FAO. 1981.

79. *Ibid.*

80. FAO. 1977c.

81. SEA. 2000.

82. FAO. 1977c.

83. *Ibid.*

84. SEA. 2000.

85. Ibid. 2000.

86. FAO. 1981.

87. Partow. 2003.

88. FAO. 1981.

89. FAO. 1978b.

90. FAO. 1981.

91. Asian Development Bank, United Nations Development Programme and the World Bank. 2002. *Afghanistan: Preliminary needs assessment for recovery and reconstruction*. Manila. Available (November 2002) at http://www.reliefweb.int/library/documents/2002/undp-afg-15jan.pdf

92. United Nations Office for the Coordination of Humanitarian Affairs (UNOCHA). 2002b. *Immediate and Transitional Assistance Programme for the Afghan People 2002*. Geneva. Available (December 2002) at http://www.reliefweb.int/library/documents/2002/un_afg_21jan.pdf

93. UNOCHA. 2002b.

94. Convention concerning the Protection of the World Cultural and Natural Heritage. 2002. *List of parties to the convention*. Available at (December 2002) http://whc.unesco.org/nwhc/pages/doc/main.htm

95. Convention on the International Trade of Endangered Species of Wild Fauna and Flora. 2002. *List of parties to the convention*. Available at (December 2002) http://www.cites.org/eng/parties/alphabet.shtml

96. Convention to Combat Desertification. 2002. *List of parties to the convention*. Available at (December 2002) http://www.unccd.int/convention/ratif/doeif.php

97. Convention on Biological Diversity. 2002. *List of parties to the convention*. Available at (December 2002) http://www.biodiv.org/world/parties.asp

98. United Nations Framework Convention on Climate Change. 2002. *List of parties to the convention*. Available (December 2002) at http://unfccc.int/resource/conv/ratlist.pdf

99. Basel Convention on the control of Transboundary Movements of Hazardous Wastes and Their Disposal. 2002. *List of parties to the convention*. Available at (December 2002) http://www.basel.int/ratif/ratif.html#sigs

100. Homer-Dixon, T.F. 1999. *Environment, Scarcity and Violence*. Princeton University Press, Princeton.

101. Gujja, B., (WWF), A. Nigam, M. Omar and S. Hall (UNICEF). 2002. *Towards a sustainable water resource management strategy for Afghanistan – a concept note.*

102. Kabul International Conference on Water Resource Management and Development. 2002. *Kabul Understanding on Water Resource Management and Development in Afghanistan*. Conference sponsored by the Ministry of Irrigation and Water Resources and UNICEF. Kabul.

103. IUCN. 1991

ANNEX E
List of contributors

UNEP Afghanistan Task Force

Pekka Haavisto, Chairman

Pasi Rinne, Senior Policy Advisor

Koen Walter Toonen, Programme Manager, UNEP Project Office in Kabul

Peter Zahler, Project Coordinator / Protected Areas Team Leader

David Jensen, Project Coordinator / Forests Team Leader

Dennis Bruhn, Urban Team Leader

Elizabeth Mrema, Legal Officer / Institutional Capacity Assessment

Patricia Charlebois, Programme Officer, Joint UNEP/OCHA Environment Unit

International Experts

Scott Crossett, International Waste Management, UK

Dennis Fenton, United Nations Development Programme (UNDP)

Anthony Fitzherbert, Wakhan Corridor Team Leader, Food and Agriculture Organization of the United Nations (FAO)

Søren Hvilshøj, Atkins Danmark A/S, Denmark

Ashiq Ahmed Khan, WWF-Pakistan

Alexandar Luechinger, Factor Consulting and Management AG, Switzerland

Charudutt Mishra, International Snow Leopard Trust and Nature Conservation Foundation, India

Neil Munro, MGM Environmental Solutions Ltd., UK

Martyn Murray, MGM Environmental Solutions Ltd., UK

Peter-John Meynell, Scott Wilson Consulting, UK

Rene Nijenhuis, Water Basins Team Leader, United Nations Economic Commission for Europe (UNECE)

Sandra Paniga, Spiez Laboratory, Switzerland

Jeff Sayer, WWF International

Fatemah Shams, Factor Consulting and Management AG, Switzerland

Chris Shank, Alberta Sustainable Resource Development, Canada

John Bennett, Report Writer

Tim Davis, Report Editor

Brian Groombridge, Report Writer / WCMC

Nikki Meith, Design and Layout Consultant

National Advisors

Mohammad Azizi, Deputy Minister, Ministry of Irrigation, Water Resources and Environment

Mohammed Omari, Ministry of Irrigation, Water Resources and Environment

Abdul Wali Modaqiq, Ministry of Agriculture and Animal Husbandry

Sarwar Abbassi, Ministry of Public Health

Abdullah Qaderdan, Director, Afghanistan Relief Committee

Assadullah Khairzad, Save the Environment Afghanistan

Post-conflict assessment unit

Dennis Bruhn, Project Coordinator

Mario Burger, Project Coordinator

Frédéric Delpech, Project Assistant

Aniket Ghai, Project Coordinator

Pekka Haavisto, Chairman

Mikko Halonen, Expert

David Jensen, Programme Officer

Ljerka Komar-Gosovic, Administrative Assistant

Ola Nordbeck, Information Officer

Pasi Rinne, Senior Policy Advisor

Andrew Robinson, Report Writer

Gabriel Rocha, System Administrator

Henrik Slotte, Head of Unit

Alain Wittig, Information Assistant

Richard Wood, Technical Coordinator

Kabul project office

Koen Walter Toonen, Programme Manager

Mohammad Sayed, Programme Assistant

Mohammad Ajmal Nikzad, Assistant

Other contributors

Dominique Del Pietro, Cartographer / GRID-Geneva

Alain Retiere, Remote Sensing / UNOSAT-Geneva

Michael Williams, Press relations / UNEP-Geneva